ALSO BY
TRACY BECKERMAN

Rebel without a Minivan:
Observations on Life in the 'Burbs

Lost in Suburbia: A Momoir:
How I Got Pregnant, Lost Myself,
and Got My Cool Back in the New Jersey Suburbs

PRAISE FOR
BARKING AT THE MOON

". . . sweet and heartwarming!"

—**JENNY LAWSON,** aka The Bloggess, #1 *New York Times*
best-selling author of *Let's Pretend This Never Happened*
and the recently released *Broken (in the best possible way)*

"Tracy Beckerman's adventures with Riley in *Barking at the Moon* give
John Grogan's Marley a run for his chew toys. If you've ever been
blessed with the best dog ever, wrapped in the slobbering fur bomb
body of the most accident-prone pooch ever, you'll fall in love with
this book. *Barking at the Moon* reminds us how lucky we are to be a
dog's best friend."

—**REBECCA REGNIER,** columnist, speaker, and author of the
Widow's Bay series and *The Snow Wife*

"Several years ago, while working at a major publishing house, I
turned down a book that I told colleagues was about 'a very bad
dog who dies,' adding, 'who wants to read that?' So, *Marley and Me*
went to another publisher and had some success. I tell you this to
warn you I am not a good judge of what will interest others. But
Tracy Beckerman's *Barking at the Moon* had me chuckling from the
first sentence and her Erma Bombeckesque style of writing had me
shaking my head in solidarity as only a mother who has had her own
menagerie of misbehaving animals can do."

—**CINDY RATZLAFF,** author of *Queen of Your Own Life*

"As a dog lover, I laughed and cried and related throughout. With the assembled menagerie at the Beckerman house, there is rarely a dull moment, and we get to enjoy it all . . . from a safe distance."

—JOEL MADISON, Peabody award-winning TV writer and screenwriter of *Roseanne, The Fresh Prince of Bel-Air,* and *Crashing*

"You're either a dog person or you're not, and if you're not, please go away. Tracy Beckerman is clearly a dog person and has the brilliance and bravery to admit that puppies are superior to children, and not just because they don't need a college fund. This warm and witty 'dog-oir' (yes, I just made that up) is for everyone who ever had a family or loved a dog. You will love it!"

—CATHRYN MICHON, screenwriter of *A Dog's Purpose*

"*Barking at the Moon* is a funny, heartwarming book for everyone who believes that pets have a special place in the family and enrich our lives. Tracy Beckerman shares her big-hearted family's journey with wit and insight."

—MATT BOMBECK, award-winning TV writer

"Tracy Beckerman's *Barking at the Moon* is a hysterical read that will make you want to run out and immediately get a dog of your own. Thank you, Riley, for confirming why thousands of people love your owner's unmistakable wit and words."

—SUSAN SPARKS, preacher, standup comedian, and author of *Laugh Your Way to Grace* and *Love, a Tiara, and a Cupcake*

"Hilarious and moving, Beckerman shows us just how dogs hijack our lives . . . and our hearts. All animal lovers will recognize the completely true-to-life depiction Beckerman captures of the way animals destroy our homes, complicate our days, and cost us a fortune, and, yet, how we wouldn't have it any other way. You'll fall for sweet, goofy Riley, and laugh (and cry) at how he completes this funny family."

—KATRINA KITTLE, author of *The Blessings of the Animals*

"Tracy Beckerman is at her absolute finest in *Barking at the Moon*, a witty, side-splitting, and heartwarming look at the ultimate role a beloved pooch plays in family dynamics. A great read for anyone who's loved a dog, wanted a dog, or even admired one from a distance."

—SUSAN REINHARDT, author of *Chimes from a Cracked Southern Belle*,
and *Not Tonight, Honey: Wait 'Til I'm a Size 6*

"Anyone who has ever owned a dog will relate to Tracy's hilarious tales of these strange, hairy creatures who delight, annoy, and love us without question, even as they steadfastly and cheerfully destroy all of our furniture."

—DAWN WEBER, author *Black Dog, White Couch,*
and the Rest of My Really Bad Ideas

"Tracy Beckerman's *Barking at the Moon* is both heartwarming and hilarious. As the owner of three furbabies, this book was utterly relatable and had me laughing from start to finish."

—MARCIA KESTER DOYLE, author of
Who Stole My Spandex?: Life in the Hot Flash Lane

"Tracy Beckerman makes you feel like you're right there in her kitchen as the mayhem unfolds. And at the center of the madness is her dog, Riley, who warms your heart as he steals the show. It's impossible to resist Beckerman's hilarious tale of life lived out loud."

—V. C. CHICKERING, author of the novels,
Twisted Family Values and *Nookietown*

"Undeterred by their inability to keep a houseplant alive, the Beckermans decide their family just isn't complete without a dog. But when Riley comes into their lives, insanity ensues. He slobbers his way into this family's heart and becomes its anchor in a riotous tale that is so funny, you'll have to pee!"

—SUSAN KONIG, author of *Why Animals Sleep So Close to the Road*
(and Other Lies I Tell My Children)

"Tracy Beckerman will have you alternately howling with laughter and dabbing your eyes with a tissue at the escapades and travails of her brood's beloved Type A four-legged family member."

—JENNY GARDINER, author of *Bite Me: A Parrot,*
a Family, and a Whole Lot of Flesh Wounds

"Sometimes, you just want to curl up in your crate with your favorite chew toy and a funny, warmhearted, relatable book. *This* is that book."

—ANNA LEFLER, author of *PRESCHOOLED* and *The Chicktionary*

TRACY BECKERMAN

A Story *of* Life,
Love, *and*
Kibble

BARKING *at the* MOON

RIVER GROVE
BOOKS

This book is a memoir reflecting the author's present recollections of experiences over time. Its story and its words are the author's alone. Some details and characteristics may be changed, some events may be compressed, and some dialogue may be recreated.

Published by River Grove Books
Austin, TX
www.rivergrovebooks.com

Distributed by River Grove Books

Design and composition by Greenleaf Book Group
Cover design by Greenleaf Book Group
Cover Images: ©iStockphoto/s-cphoto, ©iStockphoto/CentralITAlliance, ©iStockphoto/bmcent1
Interior Images: ©iStockphoto/Vect0r0vich

Publisher's Cataloging-in-Publication data is available.

Print ISBN: 978-1-63299-393-9

eBook ISBN: 978-1-63299-394-6

First Edition

For Riley
The Best Dog Ever

CONTENTS

AUTHOR'S NOTE

I have tried to recreate events, locales, and conversations accurately from my memories of them. In some instances I have changed the names of individuals and places in order to maintain their anonymity. I may have also altered any identifying characteristics and details such as physical properties, occupations, and places of occupation.

However, the events described in *Barking at the Moon* did happen because if you have a dog, you know you can't make this stuff up.

FOREWORD BY
W. BRUCE CAMERON,

Author of the *New York Times* Bestseller, *A Dog's Purpose*

actually know Tracy Beckerman personally because she spat cheese on me. I told our mutual friend and fellow writer, Gordon Kirkland, about this incident and he said, "Oh yes, she spat cheese on me, too."

So, that's the first thing I learned about Tracy Beckerman. She comes from a culture where people expectorate dairy products at each other. It's their way of saying hello. I'm not sure how the tradition started, but I'm pretty sure it occurred after the invention of cows.

Drone footage reveals she's an accomplished writer whose column is carried in around 200,000 newspapers. She takes in oxygen and emits greenhouse gases. Her parents were childless her whole life.

That's Tracy's biography. I hope I spelled "cows" correctly.

The book you are about to read will make you laugh and cry and emit cheese, if you happen to have some in your mouth when you run across one of her hilarious takes on her life. If you don't have cheese, try almonds, but I'd recommend against Cheez Whiz. Almonds will make a satisfying plink when they hit someone else's glasses, but Cheez Whiz will probably not get far past your lips. I don't know why I can't get over this whole cheese-spitting thing but I'm not making it up, as Dave Barry would say.

I know Dave Barry personally as well, but he didn't spit anything at me, so I don't think he regards me as a close friend. Isn't this a great Foreword so far?

At the time of this writing, the title of this wonderful doggy memoir is not yet set. I am voting for *The Book with a Foreword by W. Bruce Cameron*. Not sure how much my vote counts in this contest.

There's a part in this book where, and I hope I am not plot-spoiling here, you find out that Riley is actually the name of the Beckermans' dog. Riley is a typical dog who, perhaps, does a few atypical things, like the time he eats a ball of yarn and then coughs up a sweater. This isn't exactly what happens. To find out what happens, you have to read the book.

A good Foreword convinces readers to read the book. I just did a search and found that out. A little late, since I'm already almost finished with this Foreword, but I think the whole yarn-ball thing accomplishes a lot in this regard. Oh, and another great episode concerns a mysterious sock thief. You probably think it's Riley, but for me, the obvious culprit is Joel, Tracy's husband. In murders, the primary suspect is the spouse, so why not the same when it comes to socks? But here's the thing — *to find out whodunnit, you're going to have to read the book.* See what a great Foreword this is? You're coming around to my way of thinking on the title, aren't you?

I was honored to be selected to write this Foreword because nobody else would do it. And, let's face it, I'm utterly charmed by this whole thing, cover to cover.

I suppose you could say I am a big fan of books about dogs. I am particularly drawn to books where a new dog arrives and completely changes everyone's lives, mostly for the better. So, and I don't think this is plot-spoiling much, Riley is a dog who arrives and changes everything. That's what dogs are for, in my opinion.

Riley does not reincarnate over and over — that's a different dog book. But he's wonderful in every canine capacity and I know you'll fall in love with him, and with this book, and with the Beckermans, and especially with Tracy, who guides us through the ongoing calamity of what she calls her life with such wit that you're not going to be able to prevent yourself from laughing. I dare you to try. If you really manage to do it, send me a photo of yourself not laughing, otherwise I won't believe it.

So, wipe the cheese off your glasses and settle down for a fun and moving read. You're going to love it.

—W. Bruce Cameron

Author's note:

I do attest to the fact that all the cheese incidents cited by W. Bruce Cameron are indeed true, and I'm eternally grateful that he has chosen to share that information here, where it has nothing to do with this book. I also agree that Cheez Whiz does not have the same spitting range as, say, goat cheese or feta. And for the record, I'm the one who introduced Bruce to Dave Barry, but I never spat cheese on Dave. I reserve that honor for only really good friends.

—Tracy Beckerman

PROLOGUE

When we got married, my husband Joel and I promised to love and honor each other and to get a dog one day. Of course, we hoped to have kids too, but the dog was a little higher on the wish list. Don't tell my kids.

As it turned out, though, the baby came first, and three years after we got married my son, Josh, was born. Like most new parents, we quickly discovered that having a baby was not the Hallmark movie we thought it would be. For the first few years that I was a mother, it was all I could do to make sure that everyone in my family was cared for, fed, and met at least the minimum requirements necessary for survival. It was a full-time job and made the idea of having anyone or anything else to take care of as appealing to me as having hemorrhoids. (I did have those after childbirth, so I know of which I speak). Eventually I recovered enough from the trauma of having one kid to do the whole thing all over again, and nine months later my daughter was born. That was when I realized no one in their right mind would take on any more responsibility, whether it be a pet or a succulent.

Although I had quit my job in television to be a full-time mom, when the kids were three and five I decided to go back to work part time as a syndicated newspaper columnist. Things hummed along pretty smoothly for a while until our kids turned five and seven and we decided the time was right to get a dog. Once the kids were both in school all day and I had all this time to myself, it made sense that we should do something that would once again completely take over my life. The kids had been asking for a dog for years and eventually we couldn't come up with a good reason to say no, so we caved. My husband and I both grew up with dogs, so we thought we knew what to expect from dog ownership. It seemed easy enough to me as a kid because my mother was the one who trained the dog, fed the dog, and cleaned up after the dog. But as my family and I gazed lovingly at all those adorable puppies in the newspaper, I realized I had forgotten one thing: I was the mom now. The torch . . . and the poop bag, and the vet trips and the baths . . . had passed to me. I would be the one on doggie detail.

Having grown up with Golden Retrievers, I assumed when the time came for me to get my own dog I would also get a Golden. They are great dogs for kids . . . loving, loyal, and just a little bit goofy. However, my husband, Joel, had grown up with a Lhasa Apso, a compact dog with long shaggy fur which he lovingly referred to as the "dirt clump," so his idea of the perfect pet was different than mine. He wanted a smaller dog that was a manageable size and hopefully wouldn't shed too much, and I wanted a big dog that could physically flatten you with his unrestrained affection. I wanted a dog that would chase a Frisbee or a ball and bring it back over and over again . . . a dog that would run after the kids on their bikes and swim with them in the pool. But most importantly, I wanted a dog that would be my best friend when the kids left for school and my job as full-time mom was downsized to part time. But getting a Golden was a hard sell because Joel didn't want a dog that was a big shedder. Then one day while I was out for a walk, I met a woman with a Flat-Coated Retriever. It looked like a Golden Retriever, with the same lovable personality, but it had black fur, and much less of it than its Golden cousins. She told me Flat Coats are beautiful, sweet, vastly intelligent dogs, who love to play Frisbee and swim, and best of all, I thought, they matched our black furniture. She said it just so happened that her dog's aunt had recently had a litter and they had three puppies remaining that still needed homes. We made a quick decision, called the breeder, and after rejecting my five-year-old daughter Emily's request to name him My Rainbow Shooting Star and my seven-year-old son Josh's demand to name him Lick Me, we called the dog Riley.

With two kids in elementary school and a puppy to house-train, it probably would have made sense to stop there. But I am a glutton for punishment. So, several month later when my son decided what he really, truly wanted for his birthday was a tarantula, I said . . .

"What? No! Are you out of your mind?"

But then parental guilt kicked in and I told him he could have his second choice: A lizard.

Most people start with a small pet and work their way up in size. Fish are the obvious trial pet. Easy to care for and easy to dispose of when they die two days after you have invested heavily in a tank, various fish tank accessories, and a state of the art filtration system. Not being like most people, we did the pet thing in reverse: We started with the big pet, the dog, and then worked our way down in size. At least it started out that way. When we got Josh's bearded dragon, it was the size of a goldfish. No one told us that by the time it stopped growing, it could possibly outweigh the dog. Had I known then that the little lizard the size of my thumb would grow to be three feet long, I might have opted for the significantly smaller tarantula. Since we were stuck with the lizard, though, I decided if we got to the point where it was bigger than my son, I was moving out and the pets could have the house.

So, now we had Riley the dog, and Einstein the bearded dragon. With two kids in elementary school, a puppy, and a lizard, it probably would have made sense to stop there. (You see where I'm going with this, don't you?)

But then Emily said it wasn't fair that Josh had a pet and she didn't. She wanted something small and furry.

"Get a tarantula," Josh said.

"Not if it were the last pet on Earth," I replied.

Fortunately, Emily is less of a fan of spiders than I am, so a month later when it was her birthday, we got her a chinchilla.

"You got a what?" asked my mother.

"A chinchilla," I said. "It's cute. It's cuddly."

"It's a rodent," she said. "Or a coat. Why in the world would you get one?"

"Emily asked for a pet for her birthday," I explained.

"Did it ever occur to you to say no?" asked my mother.

"She said what she really wanted was a llama, but we went with the chinchilla instead," I said. "They're both South American animals from the Andes, but one is significantly smaller than the other and doesn't require a variance from our town to reside in our home. Also, the chinchilla doesn't spit."

So, now we had Riley the dog, Einstein the bearded dragon, and Henry the chinchilla. Along the way we also picked up some goldfish and named them Larry. Yes, they were *all* named Larry.

This is our story.

PART ONE

HOUSEBREAK HOTEL

truly believe God makes puppies so cute so you don't return them when they completely destroy your home. When we got Riley, he was a little ball of floof on stubby legs with a back end that wiggled like a penguin when he walked. Looking at him, you wouldn't think, "Now here is a ferocious animal capable of unthinkable destruction." But in his first few weeks with us, he chewed the legs off our kitchen table and the edges off our pantry cabinets. He refused to be housebroken and peed in every possible spot on every rug we owned. He broke through a dog-proof gate, ran through a wet cement subfloor, and then tracked the cement across the entire house, up the stairs, and across my white, duvet-covered bed. And then, while I was still cleaning up bits of dried cement, he threw up on my bedroom rug.

This was not the puppy experience we expected, but it was the puppy experience we got. I was only three years old when my parents got our first dog, so I had no memory of how challenging puppyhood could be, nor did I care if the dog pulled all the stuffing out of the sofa and then ate it. All I remember was how amazing it was to have a dog, and now, as a parent, wanting to share that with my own kids.

The breeder we found lived in a remote part of New Jersey, about fifty minutes away from our house where we lived in a quiet suburb outside New York City. Her home was a modest ranch, with wood paneling and matching laminate floors inside, a large dog run outside, and furniture that had been chewed and gnawed upon countless times and permeated with the stale smell of dog urine. There were moments as a child that I dreamed of owning a female dog as an adult and letting her have puppies. But after visiting the breeder's home, I decided that I was happy with having just one puppy to ruin my furniture and stink up my house.

The puppies were eight weeks old and were as round as they were long, each identified by a brightly colored ribbon tied loosely around their black necks. There was a male named Big Blue, a female named Peppy Pink, and another male named Mellow Yellow. The orange, green, purple, and red puppies were already spoken for by other families, and there were another five that were being kept by the breeder herself. It took mere seconds for the puppies to swarm my kids when they sat on the floor, knock them over, and try to lick them to death.

"Mommy, there is puppiness all over me," said Emily as she laughed and wriggled beneath the furry mass. "Can we keep them all?"

Her brother, Josh, was pinned to the floor next to her where he struggled halfheartedly to escape the onslaught of a puppy tsunami. At that moment, I thought, they were the happiest kids on the planet.

I smiled from where I stood near the whelping box, cradling the sleepy, yellow-ribboned fellow the breeder had matched us with.

"I think one puppy is enough, Em," I said.

"But if we get two, they can keep each other company when me and Josh go to school."

I shook my head. Two puppies to housebreak. Two puppies to train to sit and stay. Two puppies to get into the garbage and throw up on my rugs. Nope. Wasn't gonna happen.

"Just one, Em," said Joel, grinning as he stood next to me taking in the scene.

"Okay, then how about a llama to keep it company," she said, hopefully, as she rolled out from under the pile o' puppies and let them fill her lap like an oil spill.

"*No llamas*," said Joel and I in unison.

I looked down at our new puppy asleep in my arms. The breeder, Karen, said he would be perfect for us. A mellow puppy for a bustling household with two rambunctious little kids. It seemed like a good plan until we got him in the car, where he immediately peed in Emily's lap and chewed a hole in the fabric upholstery of the car seat. When we pulled into the driveway and let him out, it became clear that whatever mellowness he had displayed at the breeder's was a ruse, and the dog was, in fact, absolutely bonkers. By the time we rechristened him "Riley," we realized we hadn't brought home a puppy. We'd brought home a tornado.

"Watch this, Mom," said Josh as Joel and I worked together to set up the dog's crate in the corner of the family room.

"Just a minute, sweetie," I said, struggling with one end of the crate. It was so big, it dwarfed the dog who would only take up a small corner of it to start, but eventually would fill it up entirely. We were told by the breeder that it was essential to crate train dogs for housebreaking and to help them learn to sleep on their own. If it was legal to crate train my children when they were babies, I might have done that, too, and then maybe I would have gotten more sleep.

The breeder told us that crate training would also help keep the puppy from destroying our house. Based on what I saw at her house,

I wasn't positive this was true. I secretly hoped Riley *would* destroy the house. Our house was a colonial decorated in the mid-century modern style, which meant it hadn't been renovated since it was built in the sixties. It was a tragic relic of *The Brady Bunch* era, complete with yellow laminate countertops, pink and brown bathrooms, and red shag carpeting. It looked like a crayon factory had thrown up in our home. Having come from an apartment in the city, we inherited a lot of furniture from family and friends that was also, quite literally, on its last legs. I suspected that if the puppy ate the furniture and tore up the floor, it would be the impetus my husband needed to agree to some updating. Then I remembered that the reason we inherited the furniture was that we had no money left after buying the house two years before. Maybe the contents were worth protecting.

"Come on, Mom, look," Josh said again.

"What?" I said, turning around from the crate so I could see what was going on. Emily was lying on the floor with her little legs splayed out and her long blonde hair in a ponytail spread across the black and white floor tiles. Josh carried Riley over and grabbed Emily's ponytail and held it in front of the dog. Riley grabbed it and then ran across the floor, dragging Emily behind him. Both kids laughed hysterically and I wondered if I could boast to Riley's forthcoming Puppy Kindergarten group that he already learned one totally useless trick before he ever started class. It wasn't "sit" or "stay," but it was something.

"He looks like a caveman," said Josh. He scooped Riley up and then set up the whole scene to do it again.

"I'm not sure we should encourage that," I said, walking over and pulling Emily off the floor. "It might not be as cute when he weighs seventy pounds and knocks someone over so he can drag them across the floor by their hair."

"No wait, honey," said Joel. "It might be a good thing to scare unwanted houseguests away."

"We're fine," I said. "That's what we had the kids for."

Josh put Riley down, where he immediately peed on the floor (the dog, not my son) and then ran over to the wall to resume chewing on a section of molding he had started on when he'd arrived. I ripped off a piece of paper towel from the puppy paper towel holster that I'd rigged on my belt like a suburban cowboy, cleaned up the mess, and then sprayed the molding with a bitter apple concoction that was supposed to deter chewing, but apparently tasted just fine to our dog.

This was going to be a long puppyhood.

Like most babies, he had some intestinal challenges as he got used to his new surroundings and new food. But when he was sick for two days running, I thought he might have something more serious going on, so I packed him up in his rapidly shrinking puppy carrier and brought him to the vet.

There was only one veterinary office in town, which was fine because they had an excellent reputation and a large staff of skilled doctors. They would come to the office after hours if someone called with a very sick pet or found an animal that had been hit by a car on the road. They shared the joy of puppyhood with you and cried with you when the time came to say goodbye to your best furry friend. Even if they had been ten miles away, I would have driven to them to help care for Riley.

We only had to wait a short time before Dr. Benson called us into her examination room. She was a petite woman with a long red braid who had the strength of ten men. She could single-handedly lift a Saint Bernard onto an examination table, and pry the jaws of a stubborn Newfoundland open for a dental exam. We had already met her for Riley's various vaccinations and I adored her.

"I think he ate something he shouldn't have. He's been throwing up and has diarrhea," I said.

She felt around his small tummy. Even with his obvious discomfort, Riley wagged his tail and jumped up to lick her face. "Yes, you are a good boy," she said to him.

"So?" I said.

"I don't feel anything, but I think we should probably do an x-ray to see what's going on. Why don't you go take a seat in the waiting room and I'll take him in the back."

I nodded and left the room. We'd only had him for a few months but I was already in love with this dog. I tried to think happy thoughts, but my mind kept going back to the time when I was a kid and one of our cats ate rat poison outside and died. Riley was almost never out of my sight when I was home, or he was locked in the crate when I went out, so I couldn't imagine what he might have gotten into. But I found out soon enough when the doctor came out.

"We found something in his stomach."

"What?"

"Can't tell. It's soft, though, so I don't think it's a mass."

"Okay," I said. I tend to become monosyllabic when I'm nervous.

"But we're going to have to do surgery to get it out."

"Oh," I said softly. I wasn't sure what I should do next. Was I supposed to wait, or leave, or go out for a while and come back? I stood there and stared at her, waiting for my next direction.

"You'll need to leave him here," she said. "Don't worry, though. I promise we'll take good care of him."

I picked up the leash I was still holding in my hands and walked solemnly to my car. Then I called Joel at his office in New York to tell him what was going on.

"I'm so upset," I said. "We haven't even had him that long." I found myself suddenly crying on the phone when I realized just how attached I'd already become to the dog.

"It's okay, honey," he said. "You're allowed."

"I also feel guilty because he got sick on my watch."

"Okay, so now we know he's sneaky," he said. "We'll just have to be more careful when he gets home."

"If he gets home," I said, and began crying again. I'm a crier. I cry at movies and books and when a bird flies into our picture window and when my daughter is on stage singing with her kindergarten class. But after I got off the phone I tried to pull myself together in time to pick up the kids from school. I soft-pedaled the news to them so they wouldn't worry until we found out if everything was okay because they inherited the crying gene from me and I didn't want to be distracted from my own misery to console someone else.

Four hours later, the doctor called me at home to let us know that Riley was great and, assuming he had a good night, could be picked up the next day.

"What was it?" I asked, relieved. "In his stomach, I mean."

"A ball of yarn."

"What?" I said in disbelief.

"Yeah," she said. "We were surprised. I've seen socks and rocks and a baby's pacifier once, but I've never actually seen a dog eat a ball of yarn before."

I realized that Riley must have found a ball of yarn from a knitting bag I had hidden, and he'd devoured the yarn when I wasn't looking. I was stunned, concerned, and also hoping that it wasn't the new blue baby alpaca wool I had just bought because it would cost a fortune to replace.

"We had to do open stomach surgery because the yarn had unraveled into his intestines," Dr. Benson said.

"Wow! But the dog is okay?" I said, needing reassurance.

"He's fine."

"What about the yarn?" I asked.

"DOA," she said.

....

According to some experts, it's advisable to practice taking care of something living before you actually have kids. A lot of people will start out with a pet. But before you have pets, you might need to first be able to keep a houseplant alive. And if you find you really stink at this caretaking thing, you might even want to take one step back beyond that and start with an amoeba.

Before we plunged into parenthood, Joel and I felt confident that we could move beyond the single-cell organism phase and start with a houseplant. We were living in a seven-hundred and fifty square-foot apartment in New York City at the time and didn't have much room for anything too big and also didn't want to feel bad if we killed something too big. So, we looked up which plants were supposed to be small and especially hearty, and decided on an aloe plant.

I named it George.

"I think George needs to be watered," I said to my husband. "His soil is dry."

"How do you know the plant is a 'he?'" he said.

"He leaves his socks on the floor," I replied.

"No, really."

"I don't know. He just looked like a George to me," I said. "Enduring and self-reliant, like George Foreman. Except, you know, we'll still have to water him."

"Who? George Foreman?"

"No, our plant."

"What makes you think George Foreman is self-reliant?" he said.

"Well, he's got all those grills, so I bet he can fend for himself pretty well."

Meanwhile, I really had no idea whether George was thirsty or not. George was a succulent, like a cactus, and I had read that they should be watered deeply, but infrequently. However, they did not say how frequently infrequently was. I wondered how taking care of this plant would help me know how to care for a newborn, other than being able to tell when my children needed to be watered and if they would grow better in direct or indirect sunlight.

"The website says after we re-pot George, we should ignore him for a week or so," said Joel, reading from "The Care and Feeding of Your First Succulent."

"You mean, like, exclude him from conversations and pretend he's not there?" I said. "That's not very nice. And besides, I think it might affect his self-esteem."

"They meant not to water him so he doesn't get root rot."

"Root rot?" I exclaimed. "That sounds horrible!"

"They can also get soft rot, fungal stem rot, and leaf rot," he added.

"Oh my god," I said. "What about when we have a kid? Can our newborn get root rot, too?"

"Probably only if we water him too much."

It suddenly dawned on me that caring for this aloe plant was far more complicated than I'd anticipated, and I wondered if we should start over and work on "The Care and Feeding of Your Paramecium" instead.

I should mention here that I do come from a long line of green thumbs, so I was optimistic. My grandmother had a fabulous garden and lots of plants around the house and so did my mom. Feeling confident, my first plant when I lived on my own was a ficus tree. It seemed really happy for the first week, but then one day, I came home from work and it had dropped every single leaf on the floor. It was completely bare. I had no idea what I had done wrong and decided it wasn't my fault. It probably had a gene for baldness, just like my grandfather did.

So, the aloe plant was not actually my first plant, but it was my first plant with my husband and I thought, since we would be rais-ing a child together, it made sense to raise an aloe plant together. The aloe plant thought otherwise. Within two weeks, the leaves of our thriving aloe plant had turned yellow, and then brown, and then dead.

"You watered it too much," Joel said.

"That's true," I said. "But I learned an important lesson from this."

"What?"

"I should bathe our child infrequently."

....

Although Joel and I were married three years when Josh was born, it wasn't nearly enough time to prepare us for being parents. I don't think anyone is actually prepared to be a parent, but especially us. Neither of us had any experience with small children, so we learned how to raise kids on the job. Sure, I dropped Josh a few times, but babies bounce and he seemed no worse for the wear. My biggest issue was that he had colic and cried every minute of every night, but seemed to sleep fine during the day. After three months, when I was sure I'd lost every brain cell that didn't die in childbirth, he turned into an easy baby and a mild-mannered toddler. With his golden halo of blonde hair and his blue eyes, he looked like one of Botticelli's angels, exactly as my husband had as a baby. In comparison, I had dark hair, dark eyes, dark circles under my eyes, and looked more like Frida Kahlo than a Venus on a half shell. Eventually we got into a rhythm, I found time to pluck my eyebrows, and I began to think parenting wasn't going to be so hard after all.

Little did I know Emily was waiting in the wings to take all that and flip it on its head. She was also fair-skinned, blonde, and blue-eyed and looked equally angelic. She was a great baby from the start, but then became the toddler from hell. Her favorite activity was to hide in the clothing racks at Target when I took her shopping and not answer when I called her until I was certain she'd been abducted. She would routinely hit Josh and then scream when he hit her back, called the school principal "Big Bubba" when she entered kindergarten, and would try to flush her Barbies' heads down the toilet when she was mad at them.

Josh, meanwhile, decided that it was better to be stealthy when he wanted to rebel. By the time he was five, he had realized when I said no to something, he could do it anyway as long as I wasn't looking. He would wait until I was on the phone or taking a nap to crawl out on the roof outside his bedroom window and throw smoke balls onto the driveway below, or use his magnifying glass with his friends on the back patio to set leaves on fire.

By the time Emily was five and Josh was seven, though, I was pretty confident they had calmed down enough to be able to handle a dog and I was proficient enough at this parenting thing, I believed, to raise one.

Everyone said that having a new puppy in the house is nearly identical to having a new baby, albeit one that won't stay where you leave him and runs faster than you when you try to catch him. Just like a baby, though, Riley napped every couple of hours and when he woke up he was hungry. He didn't sleep through the night, he peed all over the place, put everything in his mouth, and cried the minute he was alone.

Still, Riley was insanely cute, and I couldn't hold a grudge when he cuddled and licked my face. But training a pup to become a model citizen is a monumental task. Especially the housebreaking part. Not that I didn't love wiping up dog pee fifteen times a day. It just made it hard to get anything else done with all that wiping going on.

Realizing I could not make my dog fit for society myself, I enrolled him in a class called Puppy Kindergarten. He made it through the first few weeks of "stay" and "come," but then was forced to miss the rest of the semester after the emergency surgery to remove the aforementioned ball of yarn. Although he never got his diploma, I was very impressed that he could do something as obviously brilliant as come when I called his name. Then I read in the newspaper about a dog that saved his owner's life by calling 9-1-1. Apparently, when his owner had a seizure, the dog pushed a speed-dial button for 9-1-1, barked into the receiver for help, and then opened the door when the responders arrived.

I have to admit, I was a little jealous. Honestly, though, it wasn't a fair comparison. That dog had been trained to save lives, and my dog had been trained to pee on a wee-wee pad. Still, it did get me thinking that maybe I hadn't maximized my dog's capabilities. Certainly, I didn't need him to be able to call for help if my son fell into a well, like Lassie, or unmask the Wizard of Oz, like Toto, or find his way home from four hundred miles away like Bella in *A Dog's Way Home*. But a little help with the housekeeping would be nice. So what if my kids haven't learned how to pick up their socks off the floor? Maybe the dog could.

I thought that if I played to his strengths I could probably get him to do something simple. The American Kennel Club said that retrievers come from a group of breeds called "Sporting Dogs." They were bred to bring back ducks and other small animals to their owners after a hunt. Had they not actually followed through, the hunters would have gone hungry, the ducks would have taken over the planet, and the retrievers would have had to be moved from the "Sporting Dog" category to the "Crappy Fetchers" group at the American Kennel Club Dog Show.

With his strong genetic background for retrieving things, I figured "fetch" would be a great first trick to teach the dog. We could start with a tennis ball and then move on to dirty socks on the floor later.

I took him and his ball into the backyard and gave the ball a good toss. Riley immediately ran out and "fetched" it. But instead of bringing it back, he dropped it and started sniffing an interesting blade of grass. I walked over, picked up the ball and threw it again. Again, the dog went bounding over to it, picked it up, and then dropped it. It seemed we had the *fetch* part of the trick down pat. It was the *retrieve* part that eluded him, a skill, it turned out, for which I had exceptional talent.

I threw the ball again and Riley chased it one more time. This time, he lay down with it and started glomming all over it with his little drooly doggy mouth. I was about to give up when he came running back with the ball and stunningly, miraculously, he sat and dropped the ball at my feet.

The ball was completely covered in dog slobber. I tentatively picked it up with the tips of two fingers and praised him.

"Good boy, Riley," I said. "Thanks for giving me the ball!"

I fingered the repulsive, wet, saliva-covered ball.

"Next time, though, you can keep it."

....

Teaching your dog tricks is certainly fun, but there are other, more important things that must happen first to make your dog a welcome member of the family. By other important things, of course, I mean housebreaking. I was optimistic that I could get the dog housebroken in a significantly shorter time than it took to potty train my kids. This was even considering the fact that my kids could tell me when they had to go, although it was usually *as* they were going.

I learned quickly that when you are trying to house-train a dog, it's good to have some sense of routine, and also…a house.

Two weeks after we brought the dog home, we had neither.

One night, a huge storm came through and knocked down dozens of trees in our town, which took out all our power lines and also blocked all the streets coming into and out of our neighborhood, so the power company couldn't come in to fix the power lines. There were electrical lines down in our yard and a thirty-foot spruce tree in our pool. We'd weathered big storms before and once lost our power for so many days that we were forced to bury our milk, cheese, and other perishable food in the snow like Ma and Pa Ingalls from *Little House on the Prairie*. But those times we didn't have live power lines on our property or a new puppy that liked to investigate everything in the yard.

It was clear we needed to leave.

We gathered the troops and the wee-wee pads and loaded into our SUV, drove over a few of our neighbors' lawns to get out, and moved into the first dog-friendly hotel we could find.

Actually, it was the only dog-friendly hotel we could find.

It was not the nicest of places, but the bigger issue with the hotel was that it was huge. It was a convention center hotel and the only room they could give us was a seven-minute walk to the elevator, a four-minute ride to our floor, and another four-minute walk to our room. You think housebreaking a puppy is hard? Try training a peeing puppy to hold it in for fifteen minutes so you can actually take him where he is supposed to pee.

All the house-training books said to pick up the dog when he starts peeing and take him immediately outside to finish so he makes the association. But it seemed that instead of associating outside with peeing, Riley was associating hotel hallway carpet with peeing. The book also said if you picked up the dog while he was peeing, he would stop peeing. But that turned out to be a myth. When I picked him up, instead of peeing in one spot, he would pee the whole way down the hall, in the elevator, across the lobby, and on me. It was like carrying a gushing garden hose down the hall. Of course, he'd be finished by the time we got outside.

Although I felt incredibly bad about this, the hotel staff seemed to take it in stride. I assumed that as a dog-friendly hotel, they were used to this kind of thing, but I made sure to have the dog with me when I stopped by the desk to let them know each time it happened so they could ooh and aah over the puppy and hopefully forgive me for my dog's transgressions.

Naturally, I tried to watch for telltale signs that the dog had to go. But Riley had a great poker face and never gave us any indication that a deluge was about to happen.

One night, Joel came back to the hotel from work in the evening and complained that the hotel room smelled like pee.

"We may have to wait until we get home to housebreak the dog. It's impossible here."

"That's ridiculous," he said, collapsing on the bed in the room which was also our living room, office, and kitchen. Luckily, we'd been upgraded to an Executive Suite, with an attached bedroom for the kids so they could have their own space, and plenty of attractive landscape paintings that looked like they were paint-by-numbers. The room was clean but in desperate need of an upgrade. With the floral bedspreads and matching sofa, it seemed tragically stuck in the seventies when chintz was in fashion and Elvis was king. The dog pee smell only added to the charm.

"People in apartments housebreak puppies all the time," he said. "This is the same thing."

"Yes," I said, "But people in apartments don't have to cross three different time zones to take their puppies out to pee."

Although hotel living was a challenge for me, my kids loved it. School was closed because of the storm damage, so they spent all their time playing video games on the hotel TV and rolling on the floor with Riley. Josh took it upon himself to train Riley to sit, and I was stunned when after two days, the puppy would sit on command.

"He's very motivated by food, Mom," said Josh authoritatively.

"Who isn't?" I replied. "You should see what I'd do for a Krispy Kreme."

"I watched some videos on TV and I think I can train him to 'come' and 'crawl,' too," he said.

"Can you train him to pee outside?" I asked.

"I don't think he's *that* motivated," said Josh as Riley grabbed a corner of the hotel curtains and tugged hard. The rooms were not expensive, but I thought it was likely the charges for damages would bankrupt us.

"I get very motivated by shopping," I said.

"I'm pretty sure he won't learn to pee outside if I promise him a new pair of shoes," said Josh.

I did the best I could, but one day I knew the dog needed to go out and I had to finish a work call. I brought the dog into the kids' room and whispered to my son.

"Here, Josh, put him on the bed," I said. "He thinks he's supposed to pee on the carpet. He won't pee on the bed."

Of course, I had no idea what I was talking about and as I was wrapping up my call, Josh came in to tell me Riley had peed on his bed. He held the dog at arm's length in front of me, as if Riley was an explosive device that would detonate at any moment. In a way, I guess he was.

"Now what do we do?" he asked.

I thought for a moment.

"Strip the bed and put the sheets in the hall. Then I'll call housekeeping and ask them to come change the bedding."

"What are you going to tell them happened?" he said.

"I'm going to tell them you had an accident."

Josh looked horrified, as any seven-year-old would.

"What? Why me?"

"If we tell them the dog did it, they'll probably charge us. But if we tell them it was you, they'll just laugh."

"You realize I'm going to be scarred for life by this," he said.

"That's okay," I said, taking the dog from him. "If stuff like this didn't happen, you'd have nothing to tell your therapist one day."

....

Once we were freed from Housebreak Hotel, I knew it was time to get serious with the dog training. I wasn't a fan of those wee-wee pads a lot of people used to semi-train their dogs, so I decided to check out all the different house-training options out there. I tried tethering him to me, crate training, and training treats, but nothing seemed to work. And then one day while I was visiting a friend's house where Emily had a playdate, I suddenly heard what sounded like Jingle Bells ringing.

"Isn't it a little late for Santa's sleigh?" I asked.

"That's Buster," she laughed, referring to her Labradoodle. "He's telling me he has to go out."

I followed her to the back door where we found Buster sitting patiently. Tied to the door handle was a rope with bells attached to it.

"Are you telling me Buster rang the bells to let you know he had to go out?"

She grinned triumphantly. "Yup."

As if on cue, Buster lifted a paw and swatted the bells to make them chime.

I shook my head in wonder. "If you could train him to pick up your dry cleaning, too, your life would be perfect."

Although I loved the idea of Riley having a way to tell me when he needed to go out, I thought that bells hanging from the back door and ringing every time someone opened and closed the door would drive me crazy. So, I did some more research and found another kind of bell that sat on the floor. It looked like a bell you would find on a hotel desk but with a dog-paw-sized button on top to make it ring.

It looked perfect, so I bought one.

For a week, we all brought the dog to the bell every time we thought he had to go, and then helped him hit the bell with his paw before we took him outside. Soon Riley started to hit the bell on his own. He also swatted it, pushed it across the floor, carried it to the other side of the room, sat on it, and tried to eat it. Not that he was a dummy, but he didn't quite seem to get the point that the bell was not a toy. It was an EWUS — Early Warning Urination System.

"This is crazy," Joel said one night as we went through the routine. "Riley is not going to make the association between hitting the bell and needing to go outside."

"I don't know," I argued. "It worked for Pavlov!"

"Not the same thing," said Joel.

I also had my doubts that the puppy would get the point. But then one day, Riley walked over to the bell by himself, sat down, and studied it.

"Look," I announced to my husband, sitting on the couch next to me. "He's doing it. He's doing it!"

Riley contemplated the bell for another moment, and then lifted his paw . . . and rang the bell.

Then he peed on the floor.

....

We finally got Riley house-trained just in time to get his manhood taken away. No one actually looks forward to the day their pet gets neutered. But you do it because you know it's the right thing to do and you don't want to be responsible for any more unwanted animals in the world. Still, when the day arrives, it's hard not to feel really, really guilty, especially when your dog stares at you after the procedure with his big brown eyes as if to say, "Really? I thought I was getting a cookie and instead you had *this* done to me? That bites!"

"What are they doing to him?" asked Emily, as we drove Riley to the vet. She had a simple understanding of the birds and bees, or rather, the dogs and the bees, so I wanted to keep the explanation as uncomplicated as possible.

"We are getting him neutered," I said. "That means he won't be able to help a girl dog make puppies."

"So Riley will never get to be a doggie daddy?" she said, glumly.

"Afraid not," I said. "Are you worried about him missing out on something?"

"No," she said. "I just wanted us to have more puppies."

I looked at the dog in my rearview mirror and felt bad knowing he would be uncomfortable for a week after the surgery. And then, to add insult to injury, he would have to wear one of those plastic lampshade things, otherwise known as *the cone of shame*, around his head so he didn't lick the surgical area. That plastic cone is a good look for a lamp. For a dog? Not so much. Personally, I wasn't unhappy about the cone. I thought it was likely that if we pointed him toward the sky when he had the cone on, we would actually get better TV reception.

I was relieved when Dr. Benson called to tell me everything was done and Riley made it through with flying colors. But when I went to pick him up, he just wasn't his usual cheerful self. Of course, he'd just had some parts of his anatomy removed, so I could understand he might not be feeling that perky. But the issue didn't seem to be the surgery. The issue seemed to be the cone.

"He's *really* unhappy about the cone," said the vet's assistant.

"Wouldn't you be unhappy if you looked like a satellite dish?" I responded.

The biggest problem with the lampshade, though, wasn't that the dog looked so silly, but that he couldn't judge distances around the cone. He kept lumbering around the house whacking things with the cone, walking into walls, and knocking things over. Our normally agile retriever had turned into a one-dog wrecking ball.

"Grab the lamp!" I yelled as the dog ran past a floor lamp, side-swiping it with the cone.

"Quick, catch that bowl!" I howled as he darted past the coffee table, sending a decorative bowl flying with his cone.

"Honey, watch out for the —" I yelled as Riley got under my husband's feet and tripped him up with the cone. "Dog."

"The dog is a hazard," said my husband from the floor.

"It's not his fault," I said, scratching Riley behind the cone. "It's the lampshade thing."

"Well, the lampshade thing is a hazard," said Joel.

"I think he looks like a queen," said Emily from the safety zone on the leather couch. "You know, like the English queens in the old days that had those big collars around their necks." Queen Riley did not look amused.

"Nah, I think he looks like a martini," said Joel.

"It's okay, Riley," said Josh, throwing his arms around the dog's neck and getting a faceful of plastic cone for his effort. "Don't listen to them. You don't look like a queen. I think you look like a turret."

"How do you know what a turret is?" I asked him. I didn't think most seven-year-olds were fluent in ancient architecture.

"We learned about it in school and I like it because it sounds like a turd."

Tired of being mocked, the dog got up and walked to the back door to be let out. Without thinking, Joel picked up the dog's Frisbee and sent it flying into the backyard. Riley took off after it.

"Oh honey, that's cruel," I said. "There's no way he's going to be able to get the Frisbee with that lampshade around his head."

But as we watched in awe, Riley jumped up, and with the cone around his head, he somehow caught the Frisbee in midair.

We all gasped, and then applauded as he came trotting back with the Frisbee flopping in his mouth and the cone flapping in the wind.

All hail the queen.

....

I thought I was being smart because we had all black furniture and we got a black dog so none of the dog hair would show on anything. Unfortunately, three months after we got the dog we got all-new, gold-colored furniture. I considered swapping our black dog out for a yellow dog, but we had already grown attached to him, so he stayed. The dog was actually the reason we got the new furniture. While his hair didn't show on it, his teeth marks did, as well as all the stuffing that came out when he chewed the black couch to pieces.

Once I realized Riley wasn't going to blend with the couch anymore, I figured the least I could do was make sure the floor did. The issue here had less to do with his fur and more to do with the large quantities of mud he tracked in on his paws every time it rained. The brown and white patterned kitchen tiles turned out to be a smart investment because they not only hid the dog mud, but also the mud the kids tracked in with their shoes. Unfortunately, the mud showed up just fine on the new gold couch when the dog jumped on it.

Even though he didn't match the furniture anymore, it was still good to have a black dog because he didn't look as dirty as quickly as a white dog. Except for the muddy paw prints he left on the kitchen floor and the couch — which he wasn't allowed on but jumped on anyway when we weren't looking — much of the time you would hardly know that the dog was dirty. On the flip side, however, having a white dog, you knew when it was time to give the dog a bath. A black dog . . . not so much. Usually we had to wait until someone walked into our house, wrinkled up their nose, and bellowed, "Ugh! What is that smell?" before we realized the dog was in desperate need of a grooming.

Eventually, I realized having a black dog when you have gold furniture is not the biggest issue. Having a black dog when you lose power in your house is. When the power goes out and there is not a single light on in the house and you get up in the middle of the night to see if the power came back on, you will not see that black dog stretched out sleeping in the most inconvenient location in the middle of the floor until you fall over him and smash your face on the side of the new gold couch.

Then you will sit up, rub your sore cheek, look at that dog who is still sleeping and say,

"Ugh! What is that smell?"

....

In order to make your dog a legal member of society, you need to get him a license. I wasn't sure why he needed a license because I certainly didn't plan to let him drive my car, but apparently, my town thought it was necessary. Since this was my first time getting a dog a license, I didn't know exactly what dog license protocol demanded, so I brought Riley and Emily with me to the Town Hall, along with six pieces of ID, because that's what you need to do when you go to the DMV.

I expected long lines, but in my sleepy town of several thousand, it seemed I was the only one legalizing my dog that day. We went directly to the window and I picked him up as one form of ID and introduced him to the ladies behind the desk. I didn't need to introduce myself because both women were moms of kids my kids went to school with. This was the way it was in my town. If you didn't know everybody in town, you at least knew everybody's business.

"Hi ladies, this is Riley O'Beckerman," I said. Riley had already tripled in size since we first got him, and I struggled to hold him high enough for everyone to see him, so I ended up just dumping him on the table.

"I heard you got a new puppy!" said my friend Cathie as she squealed and came over to pet him. "He's adorable. Is he Irish?"

"No. Why did you think he's Irish?"

"Because his last name is O'Beckerman."

"Oh!" I laughed. "Actually, he's a Flat-Coated Retriever. They're like black Goldens."

"Then what does the 'O' stand for in O'Beckerman?"

Emily pushed her way to the window and tiptoed over the edge so she could be seen.

"It stands for, 'O no, Riley threw up on the rug.' And, 'O no, Riley rolled in a dead thing.' And, 'O no, Riley ate a rock again.'"

The ladies laughed, both at the definition and the fact that my five-year-old had picked up on what we were saying and could recite it back perfectly. I noticed the dog was starting to lose his footing on the slippery desk so I grabbed hold of him, plunked him back down on the floor, and gave the leash to Emily.

"That's funny," said Cathie. "So, what can we do for you today?"

"Riley needs a license," said Emily. "So he can drive."

"Not so he can drive," I told her.

"That's what you said."

"I was kidding. Dogs can't drive."

"Why not?"

"They get too distracted when they see a squirrel on the side of the road," I said to her.

She nodded in agreement. "That makes sense."

I smiled and turned back to the window. "So, he got his rabies vaccine and I brought a copy of his birth certificate, his address, his adoption papers, his Puppy Kindergarten photo ID, his bank statement, and his debit card."

"He has a debit card?" asked Cathie.

"He prefers that to a credit card so he doesn't have to pay the interest," I replied.

"Okay, you just have to fill out this form," she said passing me a short document, "and pay fifteen dollars."

"That's it?" I said. "He doesn't have to take a knowledge test, or pledge allegiance to the flag, or show that he is a dog of fine and good moral character?"

"Just the last one," she said.

"That's good," I said. "Because he'd probably fail the test. He always forgets which months have thirty days."

"Thirty days has September, April, June, and November," said Emily.

"Thanks, Em," I said. "I always forget that, too."

"All the rest have thirty-one, excepting February alone," she said, and then turned to me. "I don't know why that line doesn't rhyme. It really messes up the pentameter."

I suppressed a laugh. It cracked me up that at five years old she knew words she'd heard me use, like pentameter. I was also grateful she didn't repeat all the curse words she heard me use in the car.

"You're right," I said to her.

She beamed. It's great to be five and think you know something your mother does not.

Once we realized that Riley didn't need any further qualifications to get his license, I quickly filled out the paperwork and paid the fee. Then Cathie handed over a bright and shiny new license tag for his collar.

As I gathered the license, the paperwork, and my receipt so we could leave, I felt Emily tug on my shirt.

"Mommy," she said.

"What, sweetie?"

"Look."

I glanced down at the floor where she was pointing. Riley had, at that moment, decided it was taking too long to make him a legally recognized dog of fine and good moral character . . . and peed on the floor.

"Riley peeded on the floor," she announced to the ladies at the window.

Cathie reached under the desk and handed me a roll of paper towels.

"You're lucky," she said and winked. "Being housebroken is not one of the criteria for getting a dog license."

....

The average person spends one hour a day in the bathroom. That's approximately thirty hours a month, fifteen days a year, or three years in a lifetime. Out of those three years, what is the likely number of days that I, a mother of young children, will have in the bathroom alone?

Zero.

While the average person may take it for granted that going to the bathroom is a solo activity, this is not the case when you have kids. In the beginning, you understand that where you go, the baby goes, even when nature calls. For me, there was a span of about four years when I routinely either had a baby in a car seat, a baby in a bouncy seat, or a baby on my lap when I went to the bathroom. If you have more than one kid close together like I did, this makes for a pretty crowded bathroom. We had only one bathroom in our first house and there were times when we would have four people in there at once. Of course, this wasn't bad compared with the time the toilet broke down and we were all forced to use my daughter's potty for two days. It certainly gave me a renewed appreciation for the miracle of indoor plumbing.

Eventually, the coming-in-with-me shifted to a barging-in-on-me and continued way longer than it should have. At some point, I began to wonder if I would be the queen of my throne, alone, ever again. I finally decided that a knock on the door was more than reasonable to at least give me the opportunity to say, "I'm busy" before someone barged in on me.

The kids accepted this new rule.

The dog . . . not so much.

The first time it happened, I thought it was kind of cute. The second time, a little less so. But when Riley started following me into the bathroom *every time* I went to answer nature's call, I'd finally had it.

"Out, out, out!" I yelled. He tucked his tail between his legs and skulked out of the room, just far enough to get to the other side of the threshold before sitting down to wait. But wait for what? For me to come out? For me to invite him back in? To protect me in case the Charmin Bears arrived and yelled at me for using one-ply? I was perplexed. Why was the dog so fascinated with the bathroom?

Then one day when I was in there, he followed me in, and because I had to go badly and did not have to time to push him out, I let him stay. As I wrapped up my business, I reached out for some toilet paper and dropped a spare square on the bathroom floor. Riley jumped up, dove on the toilet paper, and devoured it instantly. I raised an eyebrow. Then two. I had a thought. To test my theory, I ripped off another square of toilet paper and offered it to the dog. He sucked it down like it was a T-bone steak.

So, the mystery was solved. My dog had a taste for toilet paper. It wasn't me that interested him in the bathroom, it was the squeezably soft and evidently quite delicious bathroom tissue.

I went to the toilet paper website and checked to make sure there was nothing toxic in the paper and then phoned the vet to make sure this wasn't a problem for the dog.

She said it should be okay, with three conditions:

a. don't let the dog eat too much of it;

b. make sure the toilet paper is clean;

c. make sure he changes the empty roll when he is done.

RILEY THE MAGNIFICENT

Riley came to us with some papers that proved he was pedigree royalty. He came from a long line of Flat-Coated Retriever blue blood. His mother, father, aunts, uncles, sisters, and brothers were all champion show dogs with enough medals and ribbons to make any dog woof with envy. His lineage was impressive stuff. He was like the Prince of Pooches, the Duke of Doggies, the King of Canines . . . well, you get the idea. Even though we'd only wanted a family pet, we thought he could certainly be a show dog, if we wanted, because we were sure he had the genes for it.

Or did he?

"I think Riley was adopted," I said to Joel over dinner one night.

"How do you figure?" he said.

"He doesn't seem to have the same smart gene as the rest of his family," I said. "I think they might have snuck in a ringer."

We both watched as the dog got up from where he was lying

under the glass dining table and bonked his head on it when he stood up. This was not the first time he'd done it. Or the second. Or the fiftieth. He bonked his head *every* time we sat down to eat.

"Doesn't learn from his mistakes, does he?" said Joel.

"Not so much," I said.

Riley walked over, put his head in my lap from under the table and wagged his tail vigorously.

"He may not be the brightest bulb in the socket, but he's certainly the sweetest," I said. Riley strolled under the table, keeping a watchful eye for food torpedoes, and then gave up and lay down across my husband's feet, essentially pinning them to the floor.

"Riley, move," said Joel. The dog loved to be in the center of the action and was constantly underfoot when we were walking around. We were pretty sure he thought his name was either Riley Move or Riley Down.

Although the issue with the kitchen table was the most obvious indicator of our dog's potentially limited intelligence, it was not the first. Several days after we brought him home as a puppy, he looked out the glass doors of our deck and saw a squirrel in the backyard. Barking frantically, he ran to the doors, and then straight *into* the doors.

He kept this up for a number of weeks before we trained him to sit and wait at the door until we actually opened it. I thought maybe the dog wasn't stupid at all, but merely had some kind of squirrel-induced psychosis that made it impossible for him to see glass.

Wondering if maybe this was a retriever thing, I consulted with my brother, who had a Golden, to see what his experience was.

"Clyde doesn't have a problem with glass," said my brother, Rich, of his Golden Retriever. "Clyde has a problem with apples."

"Huh?"

"We have a crab apple tree in our yard and he loves the apples, but they make him sick," my brother explained. "He will eat a dozen of them and then he'll throw up. Then he'll go right back out and eat a dozen more."

"Doesn't learn from his mistakes, does he?"

"Not so much," he said.

I decided that Riley probably wasn't going to win any trophies or ribbons, but he was sweet and lovable and ultimately, as a pet, that's what really mattered.

A few days later, I took Riley to see Dr. Benson for his annual checkup. As he slobbered all over her, she patted his head.

"Wow, that's quite a bump on the top of his head," she exclaimed.

"Yeah, he bonks his head a lot," I said sheepishly. "I'm actually a little worried about it."

"No, it's fine," she said. "All retrievers have this pronounced bump."

"Really?"

"Yeah. It's his *occiput*," she explained. "We call it a 'smart bump!' He must be very smart!" she exclaimed as she scratched him behind the ears before hoisting him back down to the ground.

I looked at the dog dubiously. He raised his head up to be scratched some more and bonked his head under the examination table.

"Eh," I said. "Not so much."

....

"Where's the Woobie?" I asked the kids. "Has anyone seen the Woobie?" They both shrugged.

"Well, we can't leave for the weekend until we find it," I told them, urgently. The Woobie was a stuffed squirrel, and we all knew there would be a lot of whining and crying if the Woobie didn't get packed. Someone couldn't sleep without the Woobie. Someone couldn't live without the Woobie. Someone was deeply, madly attached to the Woobie. And that someone . . . was the dog.

Most of the time, it wasn't that hard to locate the Woobie. It was usually in Riley's mouth. He carried it around the house with him and sucked on it until he fell asleep, and then he would suck on it some more in his sleep. Every once in a while, after he had been sucking on it for a couple of days, I would pry it from his mouth and throw it in the washing machine. Then, every couple of months, when the washing machine could no longer get the dog slobber off it, I would replace it with a look-alike Woobie. When the Woobie was being washed or replaced, the dog would whine and cry from Woobie withdrawal. When the Woobie was returned, peace reigned once more. Our dog was a full-blown Woobie addict.

My husband and I had some experience with this kind of thing. When the kids were little, Josh had an attachment to a stuffed Winnie the Pooh and Emily had her pink Blankie. The Pooh and Blankie went everywhere with us and if we forgot to bring them or left them behind wherever we had gone, the kids would be inconsolable. Just like the dog's Woobie, Pooh and Blankie spent a lot of time in my children's mouths and I would have to sneak them away and wash them periodically when they got stiff with kid spit. Eventually they would get so gross I would have to replace them (Pooh and Blankie, not the kids. Although I did think about doing that sometimes). Fortunately, look-alikes were fairly easy to come by, but I lived in fear of the day I couldn't find a replacement and the jig would be up. I just hoped that that day wouldn't come until after they left for college.

While Pooh and Blankie had thankfully been relocated to the closet by this point, the dog was nearly a year old and he and the Woobie were still going strong.

"Did you get him *another* Woobie?" Joel asked when he got home and saw Riley sucking on a new stuffed squirrel. It squeaked softly in the rhythm of the Queen song "We Will Rock You." Squeak, squeak, pause. Squeak, squeak, pause. And we wondered why every time the dog sucked his Woobie, we would break out in song?

"Well, the other one was gross," I explained.

"They all get to be gross," he said. "That's what happens when he sucks the life out of them."

"What do you think we should do?" I asked him.

"Here's a thought," he said. "*Don't* buy him any more Woobies!"

"Go cold turkey? That's cruel!" I protested. "He has an oral fixation. He needs to come off it slowly."

"So what, should we get him some Woobie gum or a Woobie patch?" Joel asked. "Enroll him in a Twelve-Step Woobie program? How does one wean a dog off a Woobie?"

This was a good question, so I decided to consult the powers that be on the Internet. I searched "dogs and Woobies," and surprisingly, got a number of hits. It seemed my dog was not the only one to have a Woobie habit. Rex the Retriever had a bunny Woobie. Bo the Boxer had a sheep Woobie. And Willoughby the Weimaraner had a woolly woodchuck Woobie. Try saying that ten times real fast.

"It says here that it's not bad for a dog to suck on a soft toy," I told my husband. "It's like a pacifier. It calms them when they're stressed out."

"He's a dog, honey," said my husband. "He doesn't have any stress."

"He will if we take his Woobie away."

We finally decided to just cut down Riley's Woobie time. We took it away and gave it to him for a little bit of time in the morning, once in the afternoon, and then at night. Eventually, we just gave it to him at night. Then we took it away altogether.

Finally, he broke the habit. No more smelly, gobby Woobie. The dog was Woobie-free.

Then one night as we sat on the couch watching TV, Riley strolled in, lay down, and began sucking on something.

"What the heck?" said Joel, throwing me an annoyed look. "I thought you stopped buying Woobies."

"I did."

"Then what's he sucking on?" he asked.

I bent down and pried open Riley's mouth.

"Your socks."

....

Having a dog does not make you an expert in all things dog. But it does, in many cases, mean that you become an expert in anticipating when your dog is going to puke on the rug. This is something you can't possibly know until you've had your dog for a while and get to know, through experience, what his puke tell is.

"Quick, get the dog outside," I barked at Josh one day.

Riley was doing some weird coughing thing that looked suspiciously to me like he was about to throw up his breakfast on the rug. He was nowhere near a rug at the time, but knowing my dog, he would cough and gag the whole way down the stairs, across the house, and into the family room just so he could throw up his breakfast on the only good rug in the house.

Josh obediently dragged the dog out back, at which point Riley immediately was fine.

"False alarm," he said. I eyed the dog suspiciously.

"I'm watching you, Riley," I warned him. I wasn't worried that he was sick. In all other respects, he seemed absolutely fine. But in the event that he had eaten something that didn't agree with him, I wanted to make sure that if it was going to come back up, it was going to be on an easy surface to clean.

I locked the dog in the kitchen while I took the kids to school and then came back to find him acting completely normal. But then he repeated his coughing routine twice more and I repeatedly dragged him outside. No easy feat considering the dog was half my weight and not a particularly willing participant in this activity.

"This is getting tiresome," I said to him.

"For you and me both, lady," he responded from his heap on the floor.

I suspected that Riley had eaten something nasty outside. This is not a huge leap considering he routinely enters the house from outside, licking his chops as though he has just returned from a fine dining experience. Since there is only garbage and dead things out there, I had to assume he was supplementing his dog chow with some gross backyard snacks. It was also not a huge leap considering this had happened about a thousand times before, with the offending snack eventually appearing partially digested on the family room rug.

In the past, the problem usually took care of itself in one way or another after a few hours. But that night, the dog was still out of sorts.

"Hi Dad," Josh said, throwing himself into Joel's arms as he walked in the door. "Riley has the *almost barfs.*"

"What are *almost barfs?*" said Joel.

Right on cue, the dog did his weird coughing thing. The kids and I ran from the room.

"Take cover!" I yelled from the hall.

I heard the back door open and close and knew the coast was clear.

"He's been doing that all day," I said as I came back into the room. The kids had smartly disappeared. "He coughs and gags, but nothing comes up."

Joel let the dog back in.

"You having a tough time, buddy?" he said, kneeling next to Riley where he was lying on the rug. Joel rubbed his belly vigorously, something the dog loved because Joel always did it with such gusto. Riley had transformed Joel from a small-dog guy to a full-throttle large-dog lover. Joel was the Belly-Rubber, Frisbee-Thrower, Tennis-Ball-Hurler, and Snack-Giver in Chief, while I was the Pooper-Scooperer and Vet-Takerer. It was kind of like our roles with the kids. I had to say no all day and then Joel would come home and take the kids for a bike ride or a game of catch or out for ice cream. Of course, I could be fun, too, but everyone, including the dog, knew that Joel was the go-to guy for a good time.

He suddenly stopped the belly-rubbing after remembering that the dog had a digestive issue.

"You should take him to the vet," he said.

"I dunno, he probably just ate something nasty and it will pass," I said.

Riley coughed and gagged.

"Okay, I'll take him!" I yelled, running from the room.

The next day I hauled the dog off to the vet. I explained to Dr. Benson how Riley had been coughing and gagging because, of course, the minute we arrived at the vet, he stopped doing it. She poked and prodded him and looked in his throat.

"Everything looks fine," she said.

"Then how come he keeps doing that thing?" I asked

"Well, there may have been something in there irritating him and he was trying to work it out, just like when we clear our throat."

"Or maybe he was trying to clear his throat to tell me something," I said.

"Like what?" she wondered.

"That he's about to throw up."

....

There are some dog breeds that couldn't care less about food, and stuffed toys, and things that go in their mouths. My brother-in-law's family had a miniature poodle, and it always astounded me that they could put a bowl of dog food on the floor and their dog, Leo, would eat a few bites and then walk away. When we would get together,

Riley would devour the food in his bowl in two gulps, and then eat whatever was left in Leo's bowl, too. After that he would eat anything he could find on the floor, outside, or on the kitchen counter if it was close enough to the edge. He was indiscriminate. He was just as happy with kibble as he was with rocks. When Riley turned one year old, it became clear that our retriever wasn't a dog. He was a goat.

We realized this for certain the day Josh came running into the kitchen to find me.

"Hey Mom, did you do the laundry today?" he asked. He was dressed in the usual uniform of an eight-year-old: slouchy jeans, a patterned T-shirt, and tennis sneakers that were so old the rubber soles were peeling back from the bottom and so dirty that I couldn't tell if the original color was white or gray. Although his outfits looked casually tossed together and his sneakers looked like they could walk away on their own, Josh had definite opinions about what he wore and preferred to have a large selection of shirts to choose from each day. As with most things, his sister couldn't have been more different. She insisted she pick out her own clothes and they seldom matched. Even her socks were typically from two different pairs. She didn't care what the clothes looked like, as long as they were pink or light blue, but never orange because she hated the color orange. His clothes were folded neatly in piles in his closet. Hers were tossed with abandon on the floor, her chair, and her bed. Rather than remove the clothes from the bed, she would just sleep beneath them. In their own ways, they each drove me crazy, although I secretly loved the fact that they were each their own person. What I didn't love was all the laundry they generated.

"I do laundry every day," I told him. "I *live* to do laundry."

"Well, did you wash my socks?" he wondered.

"Did you put them in the hamper?"

"Yeah."

"I don't recall seeing them," I admitted, shrugging.

He shook his head. "But I have no socks."

I looked at him incredulously. He owned about two dozen pairs of socks. He wore two pairs every day: one for school and one for lacrosse. If he put them in the laundry basket, I would have washed them. That is, unless *someone* intercepted them and removed them from the laundry basket.

And that someone could only be . . .

The Dirty Sock Thief.

Yes, we had a sock thief living amongst us. By day he was a mild-mannered retriever. But at night he transformed into a nefarious, four-legged, fuzzy sock thief.

What was worse than him stealing socks, however, was what he did with them once he had them in his possession:

He glommed on them.

For those who are not familiar with this term, to "glom" means to wrap your mouth around an object and drool excessively all over it. And in case you were wondering, this is not a good thing. Especially if you are the owner of the item being glommed upon.

Typically, when Riley gets his glom on, he limits it to one or two socks. But it seemed he had upped his nightly visits to the laundry basket and made off with almost a dozen socks right under our noses. Additionally, it would appear he had developed a specific taste for one person's dirty socks: my son's.

Until I realized what was going on, I assumed that Josh's socks had gone MIA in our dryer, where socks went in but they didn't come out. I was convinced there was a planet on the other side of the universe where all our missing socks had ended up after passing through a black hole in our dryer. Usually just one of a pair would disappear, which was probably fine for the one-legged aliens that lived on the other side of the black hole. But on our planet where my family all had two feet, I would be forced to throw the matching sock out and buy Josh more socks. Naturally, as soon as I threw a sock out, its mate would miraculously appear. It was somewhat comforting to find out that there wasn't a black hole in our dryer, after all. Although I was convinced there was indeed one in the family room that sucked up my husband's shoes, since he couldn't find them most of the time.

"I think the dog stole your socks," I said to Josh. "I'm not sure where they are, but you can bet when we find them, they will be significantly glommed upon."

He wrinkled up his nose. "That is so gross. What's wrong with him? Who sucks on socks? Eww."

"We need to give him our compassion, Josh, not our contempt," I said gently. "Clearly, he has a problem. I think he has to admit he has become powerless over socks." I'd heard that when some people give up one addiction, they sometimes take on another. For Riley, it started with Woobies, and then when he gave that up, he turned to socks. At least it wasn't grubs.

We went downstairs and found the dog curled up innocently in his crate. I called him to come out, and that's when we discovered the stash of glommed-up socks in the back of the crate.

Josh crawled into the dog's crate and started to retrieve the mass of socks. Then he turned and popped his head out.

"Good news," he said. "It seems like he might be coming to the end of his sock-stealing days."

"How can you tell?" I asked him.

Josh grabbed something from the back of the crate and handed it to me.

"Looks like he's moved on to your underwear."

....

It was obvious right from the start that our dog was a petty thief.

In the beginning, his crimes were limited to dirty socks and underwear stolen straight out of the laundry basket. Although these would not be *my* choice of items to steal, I did understand the appeal for the dog. The items were sweaty, stiff, and stinky . . . a trifecta of doggie goodness. He would nab them when no one was looking and then create a stash under his dog bed so that if one stinky sock was discovered, there was another to chew on in its place. He was devious for sure, but he was not completely without merit. Like the Robin Hood of the canine world, he would steal the dirty laundry, and then, after they had been properly chewed, leave them for anyone else who might be in need of a dirty, slobbery sock.

But what started out as a series of misdemeanors soon escalated. From socks and underwear, he moved on to dish towels, hijacked right off the kitchen counter. Then used tissues, nicked from the wastepaper baskets. The evidence was there. There was no doubt it was the dog. He left a trail of drool with his name all over it.

"Honey, have you seen my socks?" my husband asked one morning, pawing through his empty drawer.

"Did you look under the dog bed?"

"Ugh. Why does he only take my socks?" he said.

Riley had recently moved on from Josh's socks to Joel's for some reason the dog hadn't explained.

"I guess they must taste the best."

I would have been concerned, but all dogs have issues, and compared to dogs that have rabbit obsessions and dogs that eat deer poop, stealing dirty socks and underwear seemed like a relatively benign problem.

But then one day I went to retrieve a leather bracelet off my night table, and it was gone.

At first, I thought I had misplaced it. Maybe I had taken the bracelet off somewhere else in the house and left it there. I'm a creature of habit and an obsessive housekeeper to boot, so it was unlikely that this was the case, but I looked in all the obvious places, and some of the not so obvious ones, just to be sure. Curiously, as I conducted my search, the dog followed me from room to room. I thought he was keeping me company, but after a bit I noticed a shifty look in his eye and a hesitation in his gait. I wondered . . . was it possible? Could the dog be behind my missing bracelet? Had he stepped up his daytime sock thievery to nocturnal jewel heists?

Was the dog . . . a *cat burglar*???

I thought about calling in the CIA (Canine Intelligence Agency) to help solve this crime, but I was concerned that if the dog was indeed guilty, he might be sentenced to years of hard labor as a sled dog or sheep herder.

As I pondered the options, Riley left the room and then came back and dropped something on the floor. It was my bracelet. It was wet. It was drooly. But other than that, it was unscathed. He looked up at me, repentant. Sensing his remorse, I walked over to the laundry basket and paused.

"Here, Riley," I said, calling him over.

"It's okay. You're a good boy. You brought back Mommy's bracelet."

And then I handed him Joel's sock.

....

Experience has taught me that dogs can and will eat anything that smells interesting, chew on whatever is chewable, and lick wherever they can reach because they are dogs and that is what they do.

Of course, what Riley finds interesting to eat and what I find interesting to eat are vastly different. I like to think that I have a more discerning palate than he does and he in turn must assume that I'm a freak because I throw away all the good parts. Unlike humans, there is no such thing as a five-minute rule for dogs when it comes to things that are dropped on the floor. The added dust, hair, and bacteria probably give the food a special texture and flavor that is something akin to Gordon Ramsay's Beef Wellington for a dog, but would create visions of salmonella dancing in my head. This is probably why my breath smells minty fresh and his smells like road kill.

That being the case, as much as I love my dog, I would never, ever let him kiss me on my face unless I had a large bottle of Purel on hand to slather across my face, and a large bottle of Listerine to swig post-dog kiss. Although I know lots of dog owners are happy to lock lips with their dogs, I just don't fall into that camp. I would sooner eat a fried grasshopper with hot sauce than pucker up for my pooch. Having seen what my kids put in their mouths, I probably should have also feared kissing them. But I made a special dispensation for dependents who came from me, rather than from a litter of puppies.

This pet smooching avoidance comes with cause. It may have something to do with some of the things I have seen him eat. On a typical morning, he might go outside and eat some grubs (somewhat gelatinous with a slightly nutty flavor . . . or so I've read), wash them down with a toilet bowl chaser, and then help himself to a dessert of used tissues from the garbage can. After spending a good half hour licking himself in places generally hidden from view, he will go outside, find a puddle filled with worms and then avail himself of a generous helping of worm bisque.

Not to be outdone by Bear Grylls, Riley will go outside a second time to do his business, find a dead animal, and try to have it for a second breakfast before I catch him and dispose of whatever the thing with the fluffy tail used to be. This outing will be followed by another half hour licking himself in those hard to reach places, followed by a third trip outside in search of more worm puddle soup.

Bored with the buffet outside, he will search out the aforementioned dirty socks from the laundry basket, which I assume are a little dry but tasty. This, of course, is followed by yet more licking.

(His mouth may be filthy, but this dog has the cleanest nether regions in the western hemisphere.)

Finally, dinner time rolls around — something that is actually edible — and he will scarf that down even though he is probably full from grubs, worms, moldy sticks, dead squirrels, dirty socks, and used tissues. I love him no less for this . . . But having been witness to his varied and somewhat repulsive dining choices, I opt not to pursue a more intimate relationship with my dog.

I was firm in my resolve until I found out about a doggie *mouthwash* that I could give him, which would kill the bad germs and freshen his breath. So, I ran out and got some. I poured it in to his bowl. He swished it around in his mouth.

And then he rinsed with water from the toilet bowl.

....

As our third winter with Riley approached, I pulled the winter coats out for the kids and we watched as the leaves first turned brilliant shades of scarlet and gold, and then brown, and then fell to the ground in a sudden dramatic suicide plunge. Our backyard was surrounded by deciduous trees, which meant our lawn was soon covered with a carpet of crunchy, dead foliage. This made autumn one of Riley's favorite times of year. As we raked up enormous piles of leaves, he would dive straight into them, flattening the piles as he rolled back and forth over them, until his coat was a mass of fur tangled with the remnants of our hard work.

This is not to say that he didn't love the other seasons. He loved to swim in the summer, romp through the snow in the winter, and bathe in the mud in the spring . . . which made for endless possibilities of dog-related dirt disasters in and around the house. Still, he had such a good time, it was hard to get mad when he shook water all over the furniture after getting out of the pool in the summer, left muddy tracks across the family room in the spring, or tracked dirty slush inside in the winter. It's almost worth the mess to watch your kids swim with their dog in the pool or make snow angels while your dog rolls beside them.

Yet, one dog's fun is another woman's cleanup, and while I liked the fact that he and the kids were enjoying themselves, I didn't love cleaning up muddy paw prints and scattered dead leaves off our kitchen floor every day during the fall. I discovered that my house was uniquely situated in the center of the universe, or at least in our neighborhood, so that every time we opened the back door to let the dog in, a giant wind tunnel, all our own, sucked all the leaves in from the deck and spit them into my house. If I didn't catch them and sweep them up right away, they would get trampled and broken into millions of crunchy little leaf pieces that would get ground into the rug and eventually tracked all over the house until I crawled under the covers at night and found myself on a bed of shredded leaf. While this might be fun if you're a contestant on the TV show *Survivor*, personally, I prefer my sheets to be cottony soft and decidedly leaf-free.

Then, I discovered another problem that I hadn't foreseen in Riley's love of leaf rolling. Several hours after Riley returned from playing in the backyard, I noticed a bunch of dirt spots on the lighter part of his muzzle where his black fur had faded to brown, as it often did in the summer. I tried to rub them off, but upon closer inspection, I realized they weren't dirt spots. They were ticks.

"Josh, Emily," I yelled. "Come here and hold Riley still while I get a better look at his face." Josh came up from where he was practicing his electric guitar in the basement and Emily stopped playing computer games in the breakfast room.

"Why? What's wrong, Mom?" asked Josh.

"I think Riley's got ticks."

"Ewww," said Emily, quickly letting go of the dog's head. "That's disgusting."

"It is," I said. "But I'm more worried about the dog getting Lyme disease than I am about you being disgusted."

"Is that what you get when you don't like limes?" she said. "Is there a lemon disease, too?"

"No, not lime, L-I-M-E. Lyme, L-Y-M-E. It's a disease you can get from ticks that can make you really sick. Can you hold his head still again, please?"

"Can people get it, too?" she said, still keeping her arms by her side.

"Yes. Actually, it's more common for people to get it because dogs can get a vaccine. But dogs can still get Lyme disease even with the vaccine. I give him a tick treatment all summer, but I stopped this month because I thought tick season was over."

"I hope Riley doesn't get Lyme disease," she said.

"Me, too, Puss. Don't worry, you won't catch the ticks from him, though. Hold his head, okay?"

She reluctantly put her hands on the sides of Riley's head and held him still while Josh kept the dog's body still so he couldn't walk away. I turned my focus to the dog and parted his fur with my fingers. There were one, two, three ticks. I kept counting, growing more horrified. I stopped counting at fifteen, although I could see there were more. Riley's face was a tick buffet and he was the main course. I decided against pulling the ticks out on my own because there were too many, and instead rushed him to the vet.

As I drove, I remembered when I was a kid and my brothers and I were playing in a patch of pachysandra and we trampled though a hidden bees' nest. My older brother and I escaped relatively unscathed, but my younger brother was swarmed and had to be taken to the doctor to have dozens of stingers removed. Watching Dr. Benson carefully remove each tick from Riley's face reminded me of that awful day when I was a kid, which was likely more awful for my brother than it was for me. But Riley didn't seem too bothered by Dr. Benson's expert tweezer action, and even got a couple of treats for his troubles, which was more than my brother got after he had his bee stingers removed.

"I don't understand," I said to her, as she swabbed Riley's face with alcohol. "I thought tick season was over."

"Oh, no," she said. "They are active right through the fall. They like to nest under the dead leaves where it's warmer. Has Riley been rolling in the leaves?"

"Yes," I said looking at the floor in shame.

"He probably stuck his nose under some leaves where there were a bunch of ticks, and he got them all over his face."

"I feel terrible," I said. "I failed him."

"You didn't fail him," she said putting her arm on my shoulder. "Now you know you need to keep giving him the tick treatment all fall and keep him out of the leaves. In the meantime, keep an eye out to make sure he doesn't start limping or show any signs that he has pain in his joints because that would be a sure sign he got Lyme disease and we'll need to start him on antibiotics."

"I'm so sorry, Riley," I said, throwing my arms around him. "I'll do what I always do with the kids after they have a tough visit to the doctor."

"What's that?" said Dr. Benson.

"Take him out for ice cream."

....

After the Great Tick Attack of September, as we came to call it, we all turned our attention to the next big event of the fall. By all, I mean, specifically, the kids. For Josh and Emily, Halloween was the best holiday of the year. When else could you dress up as your favorite character/superhero/movie star, etc., then go door to door to demand that strangers give you some candy, and have it handed over, for free, no questions asked, without having the police show up? The stores started loading up on Halloween supplies around Labor Day and by October I refused to take the kids shopping with me for fear of the ensuing costume and candy negotiations. At eight and ten, Josh and Emily were in prime Halloween years, and I knew I needed to balance letting them have a good time with making sure they didn't spend the next year in the dentist's office getting new cavities filled.

But then one day, I made a critical error: I took Emily into the pet shop right before Halloween. The smell of cheese-flavored treats and cedar hamster bedding filled the air, and tempting dog snacks, pet toys, and brightly colored betta fish were positioned right up front to entice you into an impulse buy.

"Ooh, look, Mom! Dog costumes! Can we get one for Riley?" Emily pleaded as she ogled the display of uber-cute canine costumes. "Then we can dress him up and take him trick-or-treating with us!"

I groaned. The first year when the kids wanted to dress the dog up for Halloween, they decided he should be a mummy. They wrapped him from head to tail in toilet paper. Then he ripped it off, shredded it, and ate it. The next year they decided Riley should be a Dalmatian. They covered him in paper spots. He ripped them off, shredded them, and ate them. This year I decided to just feed him a ream of paper and save us all the trouble.

"First of all, no. Second of all, no," I replied, gently taking a doggie Cinderella crown from her and putting it back on the rack. "You know he hates to be dressed up. And besides, there's no point in taking him trick-or-treating. I don't think anyone will be giving out dog biscuits."

She persisted, but I was adamant. Part of it had to do with saving my dog's pride. There's no dignity in being a dog dressed up as Yoda or

Shrek. Besides, I am not one of those pet owners who treats their pet like a fuzzy baby. I don't dress him in four-sleeved Burberry raincoats or Land's End argyle doggie sweaters. He doesn't wear puppy Uggs or doggie Crocs. In fact, the closest he ever came to canine couture was when he had to wear the medical lampshade around his head.

What it really came down to was the fact that I was cheap. I just wasn't willing to plunk down forty bucks on a stupid dog costume for one night.

While we waited to check out, I glanced at the display. There was actually a very impressive collection of ridiculous dog costumes: everything from Wonder Woman-dog to Star Wars Jedi-dog. Clearly someone was spending money on this stuff. It just wasn't going to be me. I'd already dumped a chunk of change on Emily's Dorothy from *The Wizard of Oz* costume and Josh's ninja warrior. Not to mention enough candy to put a small army into a sugar coma, as well as a vast collection of spider webs, pumpkins, fake spiders, Styrofoam head-stones, and all the other stuff the kids wanted to use to decorate the outside of the house for Halloween.

Then I had an idea. The kids and the dog were about the same size. The dog could borrow one of the kids' old costumes. After so many years of my kids trick-or-treating, we had enough costumes to outfit a whole kennel of dogs, and not just one costume-challenged retriever.

"Okay, you can dress the dog up for Halloween," I said to Emily. "But we're not buying him a new costume. He gets a hand-me-down from you, okay?"

She looked longingly at the Wonder Woman dog costume. "Okay."

At home we took the trunk of old costumes down from the attic. We dug through and pulled out costumes for Harpo Marx, a Power Ranger, Little Orphan Annie, Harry Potter, a witch, a devil, and Cher (Okay, that last one was mine). We rejected anything with a wig, glasses, or a broomstick, deciding that costumes requiring the use of opposable thumbs wouldn't work, and we discarded anything that could be tripped over, tangled in, or peed on. We were left with the devil.

"This is perfect, Mom," Emily exclaimed. "Riley can be a Devil Dog! Get it, Devil Dog . . . just like the snack!"

Which made perfect sense when he ripped it off, shredded it, and ate it.

....

Although I loved Halloween, I had mixed feelings about it because it marked the beginning of the holiday season and that, in turn, marked the beginning of the holiday weight gain season. This, as it turned out, was not just a problem for me. It was also a problem for our goat, Riley.

"I think Riley's looking a little jolly, honey," my husband commented as he pet the dog.

"You mean happy?" I replied. "Of course he's happy. He's a dog."

"No, not happy," he clarified. "Fat."

"Ssh!" I hissed as I jumped up and covered the dog's ears. "We don't want him to have body issues."

I stepped back and surveyed the dog. Truth be told, there did seem to be a little more of him these days. I realized with the colder weather and shorter days, he was probably getting less exercise. Also, there had been a noticeable increase in the amount of holiday treats that had found their way onto the floor. It was definitely within the realm of possibility that the dog had a little more jingle in his bells than he did a month ago.

"Well, you know, it *is* the holiday season," I reasoned. "The average person puts on five to seven pounds during the holidays."

"Person," he said. "Not dog. The dog is not supposed to put on weight over the holidays. It's not good for him. If he keeps this up, we're going to have to start calling him Santa Paws."

"Maybe he just needs some doggie Spanx," I suggested.

"He needs a doggie diet!" declared Joel.

I gazed at the dog forlornly. I could empathize with his predicament. It wasn't even Christmas yet and I was already well into my holiday weight gain. An extra serving of sweet potato pie here, some peppermint bark there, and before I knew it, boom, I was back into my fat pants.

It was the same for the dog. Not that he had fat pants. But we did have to loosen his collar a notch.

Since the odds of diet success are much better if you do it with a partner, I decided Riley and I would trim down together. For Riley, that meant no snacks between meals and a little less dog chow. For me that also meant no snacks between meals and a little less people chow. The tough part was, with kids in the house, friends dropping by, and holiday gift baskets being delivered daily, it was nearly impossible to stick to my food plan. Plus, my partner was cheating. On more than one occasion I caught the dog eating sticks outside.

I deliberated some drastic measures — a juice cleanse, the Paleo diet, the raw food diet, the no food diet — but none of them seemed like the right solution.

As I munched miserably on some festive holiday celery, I was struck by an idea.

"I think I figured out the best way for Riley and me to lose weight," I said enthusiastically to my husband.

"How?" replied my husband.

"I'm going to do what the celebrities do."

"What's that?" he wondered.

"I'm just going to take our pictures and Photoshop them."

....

We all gathered around the cake and sang:

". . . Happy birthday, dear Riley, happy birthday to you."

If you're wondering what kind of people would throw a birthday party for their dog, well I guess now you know. We thought throwing Riley a party for his third birthday wasn't nearly as bad as our friends who had thrown a Bark Mitzvah for their Jewish dog and served kosher kibble while they all yelled, "Muzzle tov!" These were the same friends who also held a bris when their dog got neutered, so I would not be surprised if at some point soon their dog became an atheist to escape all the nonsense.

A birthday party for your dog was a whole other matzo ball. It was really just a giant playdate for all your dog's friends. Usually it's just done for the first birthday and is considered a milestone in any well-heeled, suburban dog's life. But we had thrown him a party each year because the kids loved it, and naturally, so did the dog. We tried to keep it low key because we are typically very under-stated people, but it ended up being quite a soiree. There were dog treats and dog games and dog decorations. There were dog guests in dog clothes bearing dog gifts. It was pretty much all canine, all the time, although children were also welcome. Cats, of course, were not allowed.

Being a gregarious retriever, Riley had many friends at the party. But it was not a diverse group. There was only one girl dog, and the rest were all boys. Normally when you have a party, you try to make sure there are an even number of both so everyone will have a dance partner. Clearly, this is not so much of an issue at a dog party. Even less so when all the guests are neutered.

For a while the dogs ran around and played together, just like kids do, tackling, rolling in the grass, and sniffing each other. Then the party games began. There was some organized fetch, followed by a round of "Find the Chewie," and finally, a rousing game of "Pin the Tail on the Retriever."

Soon it was time to open the presents. Riley was overjoyed to receive numerous chew toys, balls, and squeaky things. About thirty seconds later he abandoned the new toys and played with the wrapping paper instead . . . sort of like when you buy a kid a large, expensive toy and then he spends the rest of the day playing in the box that it came in.

Everybody was having a fine time when suddenly, a fight broke out. Molly, the only female, a sassy Goldendoodle with a lovely pink collar, took a toy from Baxter, a pretty chill Boxer. He wasn't playing with it at the time, but it was his, so technically she should have given it up when he asked for it. Soon the other dogs joined in and before we knew it, the fur flew and there was a doggie brawl free-for-all.

"Doggone it," said my daughter, the hostess.

"That's ruff," a friend commented.

It looked as though the party would come to an abrupt end when out of the melee stepped a large black dog with the prized floppy Frisbee in his mouth. While the other dogs continued to tussle, our dog Riley padded over and dropped the Frisbee at my feet.

"Whoa. He gave up the friz," Emily whispered. "He never gives up the friz!"

Both of us stared at the offering, and then I called Baxter, threw the Frisbee, and off he ran. Peace was restored once more.

Eventually the party came to an end just like any kid's birthday party would.

The guests all got favors, the birthday boy fell asleep, and the mom was left to clean up all the crap.

MY DOG WEARS
BOXER SHORTS

The day Josh came home from playing with a friend who had a pet iguana, I knew the jig was up.

"Why do we need to get him a pet?" I asked my husband when Josh decided he couldn't live another day without a lizard of his own. "He already has a pet. Remember, 'Please, Mom, all I want is a puppy?'"

"You know Josh has been fascinated with bugs and reptiles since he could walk," said my husband, the man of science. "I think it would be good to encourage his interest."

"He's interested in platypuses, too," I said. "Let's get him one of those. At least they're mammals."

Unfortunately, our local pet store didn't carry platypuses, or platypi, as some people with too much time on their hands like to call them. So, instead we got a bearded dragon. I suppose I should be grateful that we ended up with Einstein the lizard, considering the other pet options on the table were a ball python and a tarantula, which is definitely not a lizard but is perhaps a little cuddlier than a reptile, or so I've heard. Still, call me crazy, but these last two are wild predators, not pets. Since I, the mom, had final say, I said no, I do not want a big, hairy spider in the house that could escape and end up on my face while I'm sleeping, tickling the inside of my nostrils with a big hairy leg. And no, I do not want a cute little snake that will grow to be so big that it will need its own bedroom one day and may, in fact, decide that our dog Riley would make a nice snack.

Before we proceeded with the purchase, though, I needed to lay down the law.

"Listen, Josh, I think it's great that you want to take responsibility for something. I would have preferred it be walking our dog, or even making your bed, but your dad seems to think this is a good idea and Emily couldn't care less, so I guess I'm outvoted."

"I promise, Mom, you won't even know he's here," he said. "I'll take care of everything."

"That's what you said about the dog." I looked at poor Riley, lying on the floor, unaware he was being unceremoniously used to make a parenting point.

"This is different. It's a lizard. They don't need as much attention," he said.

"Okay, just remember that when he poops in the tank, you have to clean that out because I read that lizard poops are really nasty."

"You think it's worse than when Riley throws up on the rug?" he asked.

"Touché," I said.

Josh showed me where he planned to set up the tank in his room and even a design he drew up for what the interior would look like, including a lizard bedroom and a lounging area, so Einstein could be a lounge lizard, of course. I figured if nothing else, getting the lizard might lead Josh to a career in architecture.

After our conversation, Josh and Joel set off to seek the lizard. They bought all the necessary lizard accoutrements, including a feeding tank, a regular tank, heating lights, and sand, and Josh picked out a piece of driftwood for Einstein to relax on as a respite from his harried life, a fancy reptile hammock, and some fake plants to create the perfect lizard hangout. It seemed Einstein had a larger decorating budget for his house than I did for mine.

When they got back, Joel informed me they had forgotten something and I needed to go out and get some crickets.

"More pets?" I asked.

"No, food for the lizard," he told me.

I grimaced. I was the one who didn't want any part of this Discovery Channel reality show, and now here I was, assigned the task of bringing home the bacon, or rather, bugs, for the new pet.

And I thought I had it rough making two meals each night, for my family and the dog.

Since Josh couldn't drive and the local crickets had all gone south for the winter, I had no choice but to hit the pet store and buy Einstein's dinner. When I got home, Josh dumped Einstein and the crickets in the small feeding tank and waited for nature to take its course. But it didn't. It seemed Einstein might be a vegetarian, because when we looked in the tank a few minutes later, Einstein was hanging out contentedly and the crickets were playing tag across his back.

"Food, not friends, you dummy," I yelled at him.

After two days of this I called the pet store. "Just put the lizard in his regular tank and then dump the crickets in there with him. He has to feel like he's hunting," said the lizard guy on the other end of the phone. Apparently, not only did I need to keep Einstein alive, I also had to set him up for success and stroke his male ego so he felt like he was a badass bro. And so, I did. And in a blink, nature took over and the crickets were friends no more.

Which got me thinking about all the other creepy six-and-eight-legged things that I've seen at various times inside the house.

I wonder if you can train a lizard to fetch?

....

When Josh got Einstein, I knew it would be just a matter of time before Emily demanded equal pet rights. I was adamant that we not get anything else that was cold-blooded or creepy-crawly, which was fine with her. What she wanted was a kitten. But both Joel and Josh were horribly allergic to cats. We realized this about Josh when he was five and went to sleep at his aunt's house who had two cats. In the morning, she called us.

"Don't be alarmed, but I think Josh is allergic to cats."

"How do you know?" we asked.

"Well, his face has disappeared."

"We'll be right there," I said.

"Bring Benadryl," she replied.

And thus began five years of allergy shots so Josh could be in the same room as a cat for five minutes without turning into a puffer fish.

After that, Emily knew a kitten was off the table, so she asked for a rabbit.

"Rabbits are very nervous animals," I said to her. "They need to have a calm, quiet life. I'm not sure that would be a good fit for our family."

"I see your point," she said, with surprising maturity for a seven-year-old. "Then how about a llama?"

I realized then that the whole rabbit thing had just been a setup to ask for something that she could not only bring to school for Show and Tell, but also ride on to get there.

"Think smaller," I said.

And that's how we ended up with Henry the chinchilla. I used to think my friends who had more than two kids were crazy. All those meals to make . . . all that mess . . . all that noise! No thank you. I kept my brood at a comfortable, manageable two. And then we got a dog. And then we got a lizard. And now, the latest addition to the Beckerman Zoo: a chinchilla for Emily. Suddenly I realized that when my friends' children have all grown up and moved away, I will still have a lizard and a chinchilla to take care of. So, who's the crazy one now?

My mother also thought I was out of my mind for getting another pet. I recalled the four dogs, five cats, various turtles, fish, and snake (for five minutes) we had when I was growing up and decided she wasn't the best person to lecture me. I had to admit, the dog was my idea. However, I had been under the mistaken impression that in addition to being a nice companion, a dog would teach my kids some responsibility. Needless to say, I was the one who ended up feeding, walking, and cleaning up after the dog, after which I firmly decided that we would remain a one-pet family.

Which led us to our current menagerie. Not that I have anything against pets. But three pets meant three different "meals" to make every day (with the crickets, it's actually four meals), three different poops to clean up (because those promises were the first thing to go out the window), three different vets to go to (who knew lizard doctors didn't treat chinchillas?), and three different places to board the pets when we went out of town.

At least with my kids, I could board them both at the same grandparents' house.

Three pets meant three times the chance that one of them will escape and get lost in the house, that one of them will bite a guest, or that one of them would be stupid enough to bark at a skunk (guess who).

After I saw how the chinchilla delighted in chucking his bedding onto the floor, I made an announcement to the world that the Beckerman Zoo was officially closed to new inhabitants.

Then Josh's birthday arrived. Following the aftermath of his twenty-five-friend birthday party extravaganza, he sat on the floor tearing the wrapping paper off his deluge of gifts. When he got to the final item, he held it up for inspection.

"What's this?" he asked, examining the jar.

His sister approached and read the label. "Grow a frog," she announced. "Oh, cool. They send you a baby tadpole and you can grow it into a real frog," she told her brother.

I groaned. "Who gave you that gift?" I asked woefully.

"The same people who gave me the fish tank last year," he told me.

As the dog started shredding the discarded wrapping paper, I mentally marked the frog friends off next year's guest list.

"Hey, don't those guys have a birthday coming up soon, too?" I asked my son.

"Yeah."

"I wonder if they'd like a tarantula for their birthday?"

....

When we brought Henry home, we had a dilemma. Henry was nocturnal, so he slept all day, and then at night, he'd be so hyper he was like a little kid jacked up on gummy bears. After several nights of constant chinchilla Olympics we finally had to move him from Emily's room so he wouldn't keep her up. The only other place we could set up his crate was the breakfast room . . . the same place where Riley ate. The problem was, Henry had a more than passing resemblance to a squirrel, and like many dogs, Riley was squirrel obsessed and thought it was his duty to kill every squirrel in the state of New Jersey. I hoped that eventually they would get used to each other and could settle into a "you don't try to eat me and I won't fill your face with angry chinchilla spit" arrangement.

At first Riley didn't seem to notice the new addition to the decor. But when Henry started running on his exercise wheel, Riley finally noticed the squirrel look-alike in the corner and he went all doggie Incredible Hulk on us.

First the hair on the back of his neck went up, then the hair on his back, and finally his tail, until he looked like a dog with a mohawk. Then he crouched way down to the ground, stuck his tail in the air, and lowered his ears as a low-pitched growl rumbled in his throat. Henry froze in his cage, realizing something big was going to happen, but not sure what. Riley waited a moment, then puffed up his chest and let out an earth-shattering bark, which sounded something like this:

"Eep."

Poor Riley — he was a bark-challenged retriever with a high-pitched woof, and "eep" was the most threatening sound he could muster. While his growl was a baritone, his bark was all soprano. He sounded like a tiny Chihuahua stuck in a big dog's body. As a large black dog, he looked threatening, and people would often cross the street away from us when I walked him. But as soon as he opened his mouth it was clear he was neither all bite nor all bark.

If a chinchilla could laugh, Henry would have been in hysterics.

Riley eeped again, and Henry gave him what could only be described as a chinchilla raspberry: "Pfft."

The dog jumped back, as though surprised that the thing in the cage would have the audacity to not only stand his ground, but to actually "ppft" at him.

At this point we had something of a pet standoff. Riley "Bad Dog" Beckerman stood poised, ready to "eep" again, while Henry "The Squirrel" Chinchilla glared at him as if to say, "Go ahead, pup, make my day."

Even though they were separated by a steel cage, I decided that the sheriff needed to step in to break up the hostilities before things got ugly.

"Okay, you two. This kitchen is big enough for the both of youse," I announced.

A tense moment passed and then the dog gave one more soft "eep," turned, and padded out of the room. The chinchilla "pffted" and jumped onto his wheel to get out his latent aggressions.

The Great Pet Standoff of 2005 was successfully thwarted.

. . . until Henry met Einstein.

....

Barely a week after the chinchilla joined the family, all three pets decided to revolt.

First the chinchilla made a jailbreak.

We think the dog orchestrated it. No one could figure out how the chinchilla got out, and since the dog was the only one at home at the time of the escape, he was the primary suspect.

However, when I discovered the distinct lack of chinchilla-ness in the cage, the main issue was not to point fingers — or paws — at the guilty party, but rather to find the lost rodent before the cleaning ladies arrived and either vacuumed him up or shrieked and quit.

I spent hours on my hands and knees looking for what I was now affectionately calling "That Damn Rat," but to no avail. However, in doing so, I did learn a few important things:

- Chinchillas do *not* know their names. Or they do know their names, but couldn't care less when you called them. Whatever the case, they most certainly do not respond to "Where are you, you stupid rodent?"

- Chinchillas are *not* enticed to come out of hiding by the smell of bananas or peanut butter. Dogs, however, will respond to both those smells and will eat the food out of your trap before the chinchilla can get wind of it.

- Chinchillas *do* leave a trail of poo when they wander away. But there is so much of it, you'll think you lost a dozen chinchillas doing wheelies around the house on unicycles.

- Assuming at some point you find your lost chinchilla, you will then be vacuuming chinchilla poo for days afterwards.

- Chinchillas like to hide behind sofas, and after you throw your back out moving the sofa to get to them, they will dash out and hide behind something even heavier.

- If your dog tries to help you catch your chinchilla and he mistakes it for a squirrel and tries to eat it, do not tell your daughter, who owns the chinchilla, but rather immediately go out and purchase a new chinchilla that looks the same (not that this happened to us, of course. I swear we always had the original).

Anyway, it only took forty minutes, and my back didn't hurt quite so much from moving the sofa after I took a handful of prescription painkillers. But the good news is I did finally locate, trap, and re-crate the lost chinchilla (the original one, I swear).

But then Josh's lizard got sick.

"Mom, Einstein isn't eating," Josh informed me. "And he hasn't pooped for a long time."

"Well, this is interesting," I said. "We have one pet that won't poop and one that poops too much. This is not exactly the problem solving I thought I would be doing when I earned my college degree."

After examining the listless lizard, we decided he did indeed seem to be out of sorts. Assuming our vet didn't have knowledge of cold-blooded reptiles, I called the pet shop where we bought Einstein and got some advice.

"We're supposed to give him warm baths to help him move things along," I told the troops after I got off the phone.

"What do you mean, 'Move things along'?" Josh asked.

"Einstein is most likely constipated," I said. "A warm bath will help him go." Even before I had finished explaining what I learned in Lizard 101, my kids were long gone. Apparently, it was up to me, the mom, of course, to make the lizard poo. I'm sure at some point in my future life, I will look back at the time I had to draw a warm, poo-inducing bath for our bearded dragon as a life lesson that would help me grow and become a better, more compassionate person. But at that moment, all I could imagine learning was how stupid I was as a young adult for getting so many high-maintenance pets and resolving to never bring home anything to care for again unless it could take its own laxative when it was constipated.

Unfortunately, nobody told the lizard he was supposed to cooperate, and as soon as his scaly skin touched warm water, he got significantly less listless. The good news was, the warm bath did what it was supposed to. The bad news was, it did what it was supposed to, and now I had a massive revolting mess to clean up in the sink. I rinsed Einstein off and put him on a towel on the toilet for a moment, and then, before I knew it, we had another jailbreak.

Here's what I learned when looking for a lost bearded dragon:

- Bearded dragons do *not* know their names. Or they do know their names, but couldn't care less when you call them. Whatever the case, they most certainly do not respond to "Where are you, you stupid reptile?"

- Bearded dragons are *not* enticed to come out of hiding by the sound of crickets chirping. Additionally, if you try this technique, you will certainly then have a bunch of lost crickets to find as well.

- Bearded dragons do *not* typically leave a trail when they wander away. Especially when they have just had their pipes cleaned, as ours did.

- Bearded dragons *like* to hide behind sofas, and after you throw your back out, again, moving the sofa to get to them, again, they will dash out and hide behind something even heavier.

Eventually all our pets were returned to their proper homes and all was right again in the Beckerman Zoo. As I rested my weary chinchilla-and-lizard-chasing feet on the sofa, my son came into the room.

"Mom," he said. "Have you seen the dog?"

....

Our breakfast room was a hodgepodge of items that didn't really work in any other room so we dumped them all in there. We had our kitchen table where we had breakfast and the kids did arts and crafts. Riley's food bowls lived there, along with Henry's cage, the family desk and computer, and a few plants that struggled to stay alive. There was the dog toy bin, and the kids' toy bin, and an area where everyone dumped their shoes and jackets when they came in from the garage. Truthfully, it was more of a multi-purpose room than a breakfast room, and if someone would ask me what my decorating style was, I would tell them it was Early Pet Eclectic with Modernist Child Overtones. But despite all the clutter, I loved the room because it had an expansive picture window that let the sunlight burst through into the space nearly all day, and with the sunflower yellow walls, it felt like the happiest room in the house.

Josh had a desk in his room, but would often use the desk in the breakfast room to do his homework so he could use the computer to help with his assignments at the same time. This could be a challenge when Emily was watching TV in the adjacent family room or I was cooking in the kitchen. But one morning, we realized the location of the desk presented an altogether different problem.

"Oh no," Josh groaned. "The chinchilla ate my homework!"

This might be an odd thing to hear your child say, if it weren't happening at our house.

Josh held up two sheets of paper, or what was left of them. Half of the essays had been gnawed off, as well as a good chunk of the plastic folder they had been residing in.

"What were you doing feeding the chinchilla your homework?" I asked him. "You know he is on a homework-and-folder-free diet!"

Josh glared at me. "I left my homework on the table next to the computer and it must have somehow fallen onto the floor next to Henry's cage and he must have gotten to it."

I looked at the chinchilla who was sound asleep in his little chinchilla hut. Chinchillas are nocturnal animals. Henry must have chowed down on Josh's social studies assignments while we were all sleeping, and by the time we discovered the evidence, Henry was out cold and the homework was toast.

This would be a good time to mention that we got Henry because he was supposed to be a low-maintenance pet. But this was not the first time Henry had caused us trouble. For an animal that lives in a cage, Henry seemed to have Houdini-like powers for getting to things outside of it. There was the cord to the desk lamp dangling several inches behind his cage that was gnawed in half. Ditto the cord to the clock. There was a mitten that had landed on the floor too close to Henry and lost its thumb. The sock that lost its mate suffered the same demise. Anything near Henry's cage was fair game for the chewing, including, and most importantly, Josh's homework.

We wondered if this was a natural chinchilla behavior or if Henry had learned his craft from the dog.

As a puppy, Riley was a gnawing, chewing, salivating machine. He liked soft things the most and would routinely destroy our belongings until we finally wised up and bought him some dog toys to mangle. He never actually chewed up anyone's homework, though. In the world of edible paper products, the dog preferred toilet paper to loose leaf.

It was also possible that the chinchilla ate the homework simply because he was hungry. Although, this was unlikely, too, since he eats twice his weight in sunflower seeds every day and historically has proven he prefers electrical cords to paper.

"What's going on?" asked Emily as she entered the room. She was dressed in a striped dress with a taffeta pink tutu around her waist and was playing with some kind of green, sticky slime that I was certain would, in a short time, end up in the rug, on the dog, and in Emily's hair. I made a mental note to tell her grandparents who had given it to her that they were banned from gift-giving for the next decade.

"Henry ate Josh's homework," I told her.

"He did?" she said, her eyes growing wide. "Josh, why did you put your homework in Henry's cage?"

"I didn't. It was on the floor next to his cage."

"How did he get it?" she said.

"Apparently, for a chinchilla, he has very long arms," I said.

Emily snickered.

"It's not funny," said Josh.

"I wonder if Henry is missing something from his diet that he is trying to get from your homework," I said.

"You mean like ink?" Josh said. He had the same look on his face that Joel would get when he discovered the dog had chewed through his laptop charger. As he got older, Josh looked more and more like his dad, walked like him, and even used some of the same phrases. He was a miniature Joel clone, and I often wondered what the heck happened to my genetic code in the process of creating this child. Emily didn't really look like me either. Apparently, all my genes had been saved up for the third child I definitely would not be having.

"You know, Mom, the issue is not really *why* the chinchilla ate my homework," he continued. "But what I'm going to do now that he did."

"Good point," I said, staring at the half-eaten homework assignment and the snoring chinchilla.

"What am I going to tell my teacher?" asked my son despondently.

"She'll never believe you if you tell her your chinchilla ate your homework," I said. "Tell her the dog did it."

"She won't believe that either," he said.

"Fine. Then just tell her your sister did it."

....

Apparently, Henry wasn't the only one with a big appetite. It wasn't hard to miss the fact that Riley had packed on a few pounds in his third year. I had to change the size of his collar twice, and while I blamed it at the time on his winter coat, it was clear that his fur was not the issue.

According to a recent report by the National Research Council, one quarter of our nation's pets are overweight. It seemed, now, that even dogs have to worry about bathing suit season. Not that I've caught Riley staring in the mirror with angst over the size of his thighs or anything, but when I noticed he'd gained some weight, I felt for him.

"We have to do something about Riley's weight," I told my husband. "We don't want him to feel insecure around thinner dogs."

Clearly, I have my own weight issues. It probably started with my two pregnancies, when I ate my way through nausea that lasted nine months, both times. Not only did my stomach get bigger, but I also appeared pregnant in my butt, chin, and thighs. Eventually I lost the baby weight, but as I got older, it got easier to put on and then harder to lose. I also discovered that the fat was being redirected to other body parts.

Seriously, who knew you could gain weight in your earlobes?

The good news was, when I gained weight, I didn't take it lightly. Actually, I didn't take it at all. I would weigh myself first thing in the morning and not only remove my pajamas, but my mouthguard, as well. Then I would step on the scale and if I didn't like the number it showed me, I would move the scale around the room until I got a number I liked better. If I still didn't like the number, I would tell everyone who would listen that my scale was broken. If the doctor's office had the same number (or worse, higher), I would tell him his scale was also broken. And if I was really desperate, I would break his scale so no other patient had to suffer the same outrage.

Knowing it was probably not a good idea to use such tactics with Riley, I decided to take him to the vet to see what was what. When we got into the room, Dr. Benson and her assistant groaned as they lifted him onto the examination table. The table also functioned as a scale, and I glanced at Riley, who appeared unconcerned as the numbers went higher and higher. Eventually it stopped at a weight that made even me look twice.

"Riley gained ten pounds over the winter," said the vet. "He needs to go on a diet."

"Maybe not," I replied.

"What do you mean?" she asked.

"It's late in the day and he needs a grooming."

"What difference does that make?" said Dr. Benson.

"If we weigh him first thing in the morning and I take off his collar and shave his coat, he'll probably be just right."

"No, he's definitely heavier," she said. "Does he get a lot of treats?"

"Well, yeah," I answered sheepishly. "But in obedience training, they taught us to motivate the dog with food. A treat after he potties. A treat when he sits on command. When he comes. When he stays." I realized that all the treats were probably adding up to the equivalent of a third meal.

So, I checked in with a friend of mine who had taken the class with me about the treat issue.

"Don't you remember, we're supposed to wean them off the treats after about six months," she said. No, I didn't remember. Probably because we didn't get that far in obedience school due to the yarn incident.

Since I am the person who feeds the dog, I felt responsible for his extra poundage. But, I soon realized it wasn't his meals that were the problem, but like me, it was what he was eating in between meals. So, I cut out the treats. He responded by eating my laptop manual. I let him run loose in the backyard three times a day for exercise. He responded by eating rocks from my garden. I took him for runs in the park. He ate mud.

I said to my husband, "He may be too fat for a dog but he is probably just right for a pig."

On many occasions, I caught him helping himself to the kids' abandoned chicken nuggets at the table. And their mac and cheese.

And their hot dogs. Perhaps, I thought, I should change what I'm feeding the kids, ergo, the dog will eat better. Not that I didn't provide the kids with healthier fare most of the time. But Riley seemed just as happy to steal the remains of the grilled chicken, pan-seared snapper, and vegetable lasagna I made, as well.

So, instead of leaving the dishes until after the kids did their homework, we started clearing the table right after dinner. And then I caught him licking the dirty plates out of the dishwasher even as I loaded it.

The National Research Council reports that while cats are snackers, dogs tend to be binge eaters. But binge eating was not really the issue for Riley. His problem was indiscriminate eating. He bit off and ingested most of the limbs of Emily's wooden dolls, two legs of our kitchen table, and a half dozen supposedly indestructible chew toys. Not much fat content in those.

Then there was the time Josh's collection of rubber insects disappeared.

"Mom, someone bit the head off my rubber fly."

"Maybe it was the rubber frog," I said.

"And all of my rubber spiders are gone," he said.

"Did you check their webs?"

"No, I think Riley ate all my rubber bugs," he said.

"If only we could get him to eat the real ones," I replied.

We soon realized that the contents of the house had become a veritable smorgasbord for the dog, so we began cleaning up and closing doors on a regular basis.

If nothing else, the dog certainly improved my family's messy habits.

Without the kids' leftovers, the fallen bits of food on the floor, and the food residue in the dishwasher, we thought we'd licked the problem. He definitely seemed more svelte and cut a more dashing, slimmed down figure.

Finally, I brought him back to the vet and we dumped him on the scale. I held my breath.

"Riley's weight is down," said Dr. Benson. "Good job."

"Yeah, good job for him," I said. "But the whole ordeal stressed me out so much that I put on five pounds."

....

Although the dog lost some weight, he was still sporting a sizable gut. Not only that, but he also developed a pretty significant case of flatulence. Yes, Riley was fat and farty and we didn't know why.

As a dog with his fair share of allergies, Riley was on a pretty strict diet of hypoallergenic dog food. After a series of ear infections, we had him tested and found out he was allergic to dust, grass, pollen, trees, mold, beef, dairy, wheat, eggs, chicken, and human dander. Yes, he was allergic to us. So, twice a day he got a cup and a half of special hypoallergenic dog chow that cost so much money it made my kids' orthodontia bills look like a bargain. Because he was on such a regimented diet, he should have been able to sustain a healthy weight. The problem was, whenever he strayed from his diet, it upset his system. And by the look of him and the smell of things, he was straying again, big time.

The question was, where? How? What was he getting into and chowing down on? The kids didn't feed him. My husband didn't feed him. Unless the neighbor was sneaking the dog snacks, I just couldn't see how Riley was getting extra food.

At first, I suspected that he might be getting into the garbage. But upon further investigation I realized it was impossible for the dog to get access. We have one of those stainless steel garbage cans with a heavy lid that you can only open by stepping on the foot pedal at the base of the can. Only when the can was overstuffed and the lid askew could Riley make a treat of the garbage. We learned our lesson the last time that happened and the dog ate the entire contents of the garbage, and then threw up the entire contents of the garbage. This was when I understood why the carpet cleaner is called Resolve. Because once you go through cleaning up a mess of that magnitude, you resolve never, ever to do it again.

"Maybe he's eating something outside?" said Joel. We usually let the dog out back to do his business and run around, so it was possible that he was getting into something we weren't aware of outside. But when I did a survey of the property, all I found were sticks, rocks, and leaves, none of which I thought had a particularly high calorie count or flatulence-inducing capacity.

"Maybe he has a secret stash somewhere," said Josh.

That was typically Emily's move. More than once I'd gone through her drawers and closets while she was at camp to find half-eaten bags of corn chips and popcorn that had mysteriously disappeared from the pantry. Josh thought that the dog might be stealing food from the pantry and hiding it somewhere in the house, like Emily. But I thought if that were the case, the stash would start to smell, and the only thing that smelled was the dog.

"Maybe he did figure out how to open the garbage can," said Emily. Our dog was crafty, but if he'd figured out how to step on the foot pedal, open the lid, and keep his foot on the pedal while he stuck his head in the can, I was going to get him an agent.

Then one day, I was home alone with the dog and I went upstairs to take a nap. When I came downstairs an hour later, I must have been very quiet because the dog didn't hear me. But I saw him. From the base of the stairs I looked across the house into the kitchen and there he was, with one foot on the pedal of the garbage can, the lid wide open, and his head in the garbage, chowing down.

Shaking my head in disbelief, I went into the kitchen, picked up the phone and called my husband.

"I solved the mystery of the fat and farty dog," I said. "He figured out how to open the kitchen garbage can."

"No way," Joel shouted in disbelief. "So what are you going to do?"

"Um, turn the garbage around, I guess, so he can't step on the pedal . . ." I said.

" . . . and call Oprah."

....

Once we solved the garbage problem, we thought we would be done with the sometimes-suffocating noxious assault Riley's gastrointestinal attacks had on our family. But unfortunately, that was not the case. It was a mystery to us how someone so relatively small in size could create an odor so bad it made hydrogen sulfide smell like lilies. Dr. Benson said some breeds are gassier than others, but she suggested we try switching his dog food again to something more easily digestible to see if it helped.

According to Dogster.com, the top five gassiest dog breeds are the Bulldog, the German Shepherd, the Mastiff, the Boxer, and the Labrador Retriever. As a Flat-Coated Retriever, Riley didn't even make the top ten, which was seriously stunning to me considering the award-winning gas he passed. I couldn't imagine owning two of these breeds at the same time without having a NASA Decontamination Unit to escape to in the house.

Meanwhile, back at Stink Central, things were so bad I was sure the neighbors could smell it wafting over from our house. I wouldn't blame them if they put their house on the market because of it. I was afraid to light our grill to make dinner for fear that our house would instantly combust. The dog was emitting such bad farts they could flatten a World Wrestling Federation champion.

It was clear that something had to be done. As far as I knew, no one had ever died from dog gas asphyxia, but I didn't want to be the first family to disprove this theory.

I got the new dog food the vet prescribed, and then picked up a product called Beano for intestinal gas, which was safe for dogs but seemed to have little effect on Riley. Then we tried GasX, Pepto, and a whole host of other anti-flatulence medications that did nothing at all, leaving me to conclude that nothing short of a giant cork would solve the problem.

Then one morning I woke up, went down to feed the dog and noticed . . . nothing. There was no bad smell. No noxious odors. No searing stenches. I quickly checked to make sure the dog was still, in fact, alive (which he was) and then I ran to share the good news with my husband.

"Hey, come downstairs," I said to him. "Riley's gas has magically disappeared. The house doesn't smell!"

"Really?" he asked, following me down to the kitchen. He quickly buried his nose in his bathrobe. "Honey, are you crazy? . . . it stinks down here!"

I furrowed my brow and inhaled deeply. Then I realized that I couldn't inhale because my nose was completely stuffed up. In my excitement over the lack of smell, I hadn't realized I was actually congested and couldn't smell a thing.

I sneezed twice and suddenly realized I had the beginnings of a whopper of a cold.

"Oh man, I'm getting sick," I groaned. "That's why I couldn't smell the dog farts."

"Sorry, honey," he said. Then he pinched his nose. "If I'm lucky, maybe I'll catch your cold."

At this point I not only felt bad for us, I also felt bad for the dog. I'm sure it was uncomfortable for him to have all that gas, even if he was passing most of it. I was also worried no one was ever going to want to visit us again because our house smelled like a Superfund site.

"Changing Riley's food has not helped with his gas," I said to Dr. Benson over the phone. "Any other ideas?"

"It's still probably the food. It can take two weeks for his tummy to adjust to the new kibble."

"Oh boy," I said. "What do we do until then?"

"Breathe through your mouth."

....

There is a little-known law of the universe that says just when you think you've checked everything off your to-do list, your dog will roll in something horrifyingly disgusting and you will have to squeeze in a trip to the dog groomer. This usually happens when you have just had your rugs cleaned, placed a new piece of furniture in the living room, or are dressed to go somewhere nice because, immediately upon rolling in the disgusting thing, the dog will then rub against the rug, the furniture, and you.

Such was the case one morning as I got ready to go to a luncheon and I let the dog out back for his morning constitutional. When I let him back in, an aroma of something foul followed him through the door. He walked into the kitchen and sat down, happy as a pig in slop, which was an apt analogy. He looked satisfied while a noxious odor wafted into the air around him. It was like a cross between a toxic waste dump and a festering swamp. It was so bad my eyes began to cloud over and my eyebrows started to fall out of their follicles.

Having been down the mysterious, smelly, stinky dog road several times before, I was not thrilled that we had a new doggy odor problem to contend with. I could not even venture to guess what the culprit was, but clearly it was in my backyard. Based on how the dog smelled, it was so bad I was afraid FEMA was going to have to send in a crew wearing full hazmat suits to clean it up.

This would not be the first time the dog had discovered something nasty in our backyard. One time he unearthed a dead, fossilized animal that looked like it might have been from the Paleolithic age, and after he rolled on it a few dozen times, he brought it to the back door as a hostess gift for me. Then there was the time we realized he had dug up what looked like an old hamster cemetery in the way back of the property that had been created by the last homeowners . . . and ate what was left there.

We secretly hoped that he might dig up a buried treasure one day, or the final resting place of Jimmy Hoffa. But so far, all he had to show for his backyard adventures were a souvenir saber-toothed tiger carcass and a couple of hamster bones.

This time around, I was fairly confident that there was a dead thing in the backyard that was not from the Stone Age and was not a missing labor union leader, and the dog had rolled in it. This meant that

a. I had to take the dog to get cleaned up, and

b. I had to find the dead thing in the backyard and dispose of it.

And in case you were wondering where my husband was when all this was taking place — he was out of town. He was, in fact, usually out of town when one of the kids got sick or when the dog rolled in something disgusting outside. That is another law of universe: Anything that can go wrong while your husband is out of town, will. Not surprisingly, these two laws usually happened in tandem.

Once the dog came into the house and I realized what had happened, I called the groomer for an appointment and then quickly ushered Riley back out of the house so the stink wouldn't seep into the walls. Then I turned to the dog.

"Okay, Riley. Where's the icky thing? Come on, fetch! Fetch the icky thing!" I hoped he would lead me to the source of the stink. But he looked at me quizzically and then went for the Frisbee.

According to a leading canine researcher at the University of British Columbia, dogs can understand an average of one hundred fifty words. The really smart breeds can learn up to two hundred fifty. I wasn't sure what Riley's capability was, but it appeared that "icky thing" was not part of his vocabulary.

"Not Frisbee! Icky thing! Ick-ee!!" I clarified.

Clearly the fetch concept was not going to work. And "show me the disgusting thing you rolled in" was not in his repertoire, either. I threw Sir Stinkalot his toy, and then started wandering the backyard to look around. I hadn't walked far when suddenly I saw the dog stop, drop, and roll.

I called him over, and then, hesitantly, I walked over to what I could smell was the scene of the crime. There on the ground was a former animal of unknown origin, now nothing more than a flattened animal pancake with a long tail.

It was bigger than a squirrel and smaller than a breadbox, which incidentally is kind of a stupid comparison because no one I know has a breadbox, so I'll just say it was smaller than a cat.

I finally decided the dead animal had, at some point, been a live opossum. I poked it with the toe of my boot to make sure it was really dead and it wasn't just playing possum. But as they say in Munchkinland, it wasn't only merely dead, it was really most sincerely dead.

As far as I could tell, there didn't seem to be anything wrong with it . . . aside from the fact that it was dead. The biggest issue, though, was not that it was dead, but that there was no one to remove it but me.

I locked the dog in the pool area temporarily and then went inside, put on rubber gloves, a ski mask, and a biohazard suit I happened to have lying around the house for just such a chore, and went back outside.

I nudged the opossum with the toe of my boot again, but it didn't budge. I nudged harder, and nothing happened. This was when I realized that the opossum was actually fossilized. It occurred to me that the opossum may have been there, at the edge of my backyard, dead, for quite some time because it was frozen to the ground.

Now I had two problems. The dog stank and the dead opossum was glued to the ground.

I thought for a minute and then went into the shed and got a big shovel. I jammed it under the opossum and heaved, but nothing happened. Then I threw all my weight on the shovel. This time the dead possum lifted out of the ground, into the air, and in a perfect arc, flew over my fence into the neighbors' backyard.

Problem solved.

....

Somehow, as he was out surveying the vastness of his kingdom in our backyard, Riley got a nasty scratch on his inner thigh. We'd only just put the Great Dog Gas Attack of the New Millennium behind us when I had to take him back to the vet.

"That's a pretty nasty cut," said Dr. Benson as she examined Riley's leg. We'd been there so often lately, I wondered if we could get an examination room named after Riley. I thought The Riley Room had a nice ring to it and I figured we'd already paid tenfold for the cost of the plaque.

"What do you think happened?" I said.

"There are some tiny splinters in here," she said. "You have a wooded backyard, right?"

I nodded yes.

"I suspect he caught his thigh on a low branch or something like that. I'm going to clean it out and you'll need to apply some ointment to it a few times a day. He's also going to have to wear a cone so he doesn't lick it."

I shook my head. Riley was not a fan of the lampshade cone, so I asked Dr. Benson if there were any other options. "Well, they have these things that look like a life preserver to go around his neck," she said. "Or you can try giving him a pair of boxer shorts to go around his bottom."

I snorted. "What if he's more of a briefs guy than a boxer shorts dog?"

"Whatever works," she said. "I just think *your* underwear probably won't give him enough coverage."

"Well, it doesn't give me enough coverage, either," I said.

When we got home, I went into Josh's room and took a pair of his boxer shorts from his underwear drawer. Josh and Riley were about the same size, so I thought Josh's would be a better fit than a pair of Joel's boxer shorts. I wrestled them onto the dog and then pulled his tail through the pee hole. Then I burst out laughing.

"Oh Riley, you're a good sport," I said to him as he stood there in a pair of green boxer shorts with soccer balls on them and a fading sense of dignity.

The boxer shorts were not a particularly good look for a retriever . . . nor, I imagined, for any dog for that matter. But I suppose, as far as dog couture goes, it was not as bad as some of the outfits other people dressed their dogs in: the puppy puffer jackets, the canine capelets, and the doggie dancewear. I knew what it was like to be a slave to fashion and suffer through trends like super low jeans and stirrup pants, but at least those were choices I made, unfortunate as they were. I don't think any dog in his right mind would ask to wear a doggie motorcycle jacket and goggles, no matter how cool he might look on the back of a Harley.

It's a safe bet that these dogs are probably the ones that eventually maul their owners.

The funny thing is, not only did Riley not mind the boxers, he actually seemed to like them. After I put them on him, I noticed he had a little extra bounce in his step and a swagger in his strut. The dog clearly dug his shorts.

When Josh got home from school, however, he was not quite as thrilled that his boxers were being worn by the family pet.

"What's the problem?" I asked him when I saw him brooding. "I promise I'll wash them before I give them back to you."

"I'm not wearing those after the dog wore them," he said.

"You didn't hear him complain about wearing *your* used boxers, did you?" I said.

He frowned. "Yeah. Okay. Whatever. But I don't want him wearing them in public."

"Why?"

He thought for a minute. "Well, if he goes out in just boxers, he might get cited for indecent exposure."

I laughed. "Why would he get stopped for wearing boxers when most of the time he doesn't wear anything at all?"

"Yeah, well, how would you like it if he wore your underwear?"

"He can't wear my underwear."

"Why not?"

"I don't think he would be comfortable in a thong."

He made a face. "Ew, Mom. TMI."

"Look, I'm sorry Riley has to wear your boxers, but the vet said it was necessary and you are the only one in the house with boxer shorts that are the right size."

Upon hearing his name, Riley came bounding over, his tail wagging vigorously out the hole in the shorts.

Josh couldn't help but laugh.

"Fine, he can wear my shorts," he said. "But could you do me one favor?"

"What's that?" I asked.

"Could you cut my name tag off them?"

HERE'S TO MUD
IN YOUR DOG

Every spring, April showers not only bring May flowers, they also turn my backyard into a muddy swamp. During this period, we are forced to keep a laundry basket of rags by the back door so we can intercept the dog on his way back into the house, wrestle him to the ground, and sandblast his paws before he does a muddy cha-cha-cha through the family room. If we are lucky, this ritual will only last until we hit summer and everything dries out. If we are unlucky, it can go all the way until winter, when the ground freezes.

Sadly, this year the April showers kept right on showering into May, which meant I had to wipe the dog's four paws roughly six times a day, for going on seventy-five days. And those are just the times I actually caught him. Years later, someone would invent a washing device for your dog's paws that did what I had to do but with a lot less effort, and I'm sure the person who did it was a mom. She also probably made a fortune from her invention. Clearly, I missed the boat.

Anyway, this brings us to the muddy cha-cha-cha in the family room.

"Tell me again why I insisted on getting a dog," I asked Joel as I surveyed the expansive display of dirty paw prints all across the floor and rug.

"You said it would bring more love into the house," he echoed my words back to me.

"Yeah, well, I'm not really feelin' the love right now," I responded, giving my muddy dog the hairy eyeball.

As much as I usually adored Riley, I was growing weary of adding daily paw-wiping, floor-mopping, and towel-washing to my job description. So, after three-plus years of this routine, I finally decided that I needed to smarten up.

I'm nothing if not a quick learner.

I got out one of my old rectangular windowsill flower pots and filled it with water. Then I put it out next to the back door. The next time the dog did his mud dance outside, I stopped him on the way in and dunked each paw in the flower pot. Then I dried his paws on the way in the door. Of course, it added an extra step to the de-muddifying process, but it made for a lot fewer disgusting rags to wash.

The new procedure was working like a charm. I was thrilled. Then about a week into the Great Beckerman Mud Plan, just as the dog was trotting back to the house, someone rang the front doorbell. The dog heard the bell and came charging toward the back door at top speed. In a flash, the dog ran straight into my paw washing station and knocked it over, spilling a torrent of muddy water in through the door and across my family room rug. Then he jumped over the washing station, into the house, and across the rug with his muddy paws to greet whoever was at the front door.

I stood stunned.

"Mom, someone's at the door," yelled my daughter.

"Who is it?" I yelled back as I surveyed the wreckage that had previously been my family room rug.

"Someone is collecting items for the needy," she said.

I shook my head. "Ask them if they'll take a dog."

....

Riley doesn't like to ride in cars. At first, I thought it was a commentary on my driving, but soon I realized that he didn't like to ride in any car, with any driver.

"What dog doesn't like to stick his head out the window of a moving car, tongue hanging, tail wagging, without a doggone care in the world?" I wondered aloud.

Riley raised a paw.

"That's very un-doglike of you," I told him.

It had been that way since he was a puppy. Nothing happened that could have traumatized him. He never saw the movie *Christine*. Nor had he ever fallen out of the car or received a ticket for recklessly hanging his tongue out of the window. According to Dr. Benson, he just had acute car anxiety for whatever reason. I could understand how he felt. Even though I'd never had a bad encounter, I felt the same way about spiders.

This went on for three years. We hoped that at some point his natural instincts would kick in and he would remember how to dog, but eventually we had to give up the dream and realize that when it came to riding in cars, our dog was a scaredy cat. We didn't want his car anxiety to keep us from taking him on cool road trips with us, though, so I asked Dr. Benson for a mild sedative to take the edge off. Oh, and I got a prescription for the dog, too. She told me I would have to get it filled at a regular pharmacy since they didn't carry doggie downers at the vet's office.

"I'm picking up a prescription for my dog," I told the employee behind the pharmacy desk at my local drug store.

"Patient's name?" he asked.

"Riley Beckerman."

"Date of birth?" he asked.

"I don't know," I said truthfully. "I mean, I know the month and year, but not the actual day."

He looked up from the computer. "You don't know your son's birthdate?"

"He's not my son. He's my dog," I said.

He typed some information into the computer. "Your son is not in the system," he said.

"He's not my son. He's my dog," I said again.

"Well, we still have to put him into the system before we can fill the prescription," he said authoritatively. He was about nineteen and looked like he was merely biding his time until he could go do something really important like kill zombies on his video game. The whole thing didn't make sense to me since I wasn't going through insurance for Riley's meds, and also because, you know, it was for a dog, but I thought if it made the process go faster, I didn't really care.

"Okay," I agreed.

"Male or female?" he inquired.

"Male."

"Known allergies?" He continued.

"Um, he's allergic to chicken and lamb."

"What reaction does he have?"

"He gets gas and the hair on his tail falls out." I said.

He looked up from the computer again.

"Your son has a tail?"

"He's. A. *Dog*," I repeated.

"Your son is a dog?"

I sighed. "Yes. He's a big furry dog that drinks out of the toilet and licks himself in inappropriate places. But I love him anyway because he's mine."

The drug store employee looked up from his computer and shrugged. "Okay, we're all set. Your son's prescription will be ready for pickup in half an hour. Will there be anything else?"

"Yes, I'd like a box of jerky treats."

"Sure," he said. "Is that for your son or your dog?"

....

One of our favorite family traditions happens every May when we open the pool. The water is frigid and the air temperature is still cool but we all jump into the pool with our clothes on anyway. I'm not sure how it started . . . I think someone (Josh) probably pushed someone else (Emily) into the pool and then another someone (Me) pushed the first someone (Josh) into the pool to get even. I'm nothing if not a fair mother.

After a miserably cold winter, we were all excited to get back into warm weather activities. Even Riley seemed lighter. At least his mood seemed lighter. His body was another story.

"Riley is overweight again," Dr. Benson said to me.

This was not actually news to me, since I was the one who lifted him out of the car when he refused to get out because, somehow, he knew he was going to get weighed at the vet and the food party would soon be over.

But when I plunked him down on her examination table/scale, the truth was spelled out in triple digits for all of us to see.

"How did he gain so much weight?" she asked me accusingly.

"It may have been the fact that he was completely inactive all winter or maybe it was the extra servings of garbage he ate nightly from the can," I surmised.

We thought we had licked that problem, but somehow our dog, the one who couldn't figure out how not to bump his head on the table, was a Mensa genius when it came to getting into the garbage.

So, Riley was fat and happy and couldn't care less if he had put on a few extra pounds because

1. He doesn't have to worry about bathing suit season, and

2. He is a dog (which would also explain #1).

However, the vet gave me a long laundry list of horrible health consequences that could befall the dog as a result of his additional bulk, and she suggested Riley be put on a diet.

I immediately cut down on his portions and switched him to a dog food for fat canines. Then I started taking him for extra long walks, or more accurately, he started taking me for drags. But even with all our efforts, he still only lost two pounds.

Then one day when we were hanging out outside, someone happened to throw the dog the Frisbee and it landed in the pool. Riley contemplated the floating Frisbee, and then he soared into the air and jumped into the pool. We were stunned. For four years he had barely dipped a toe in the water, which we found surprising since he was supposed to be a dog that loved water. We didn't push him, though, because he already had car anxiety and I didn't want to give him something else to be anxious about. But something about the Frisbee landing in the pool broke through whatever misgivings he had and once he dove in, he became the Michael Phelps of retrievers. Every day he would dash outside, drop his Frisbee in the pool, and jump in to get it. He did this over and over again, logging about fifty laps of doggie freestyle a day. Within three weeks, he was the trimmest he'd ever been.

"He looks amazing!" Dr. Benson said when I brought the dog in again. "How did you do it?"

"I didn't do it," I said. "He did it. He took up swimming."

"That's great," she said. "He really looks so fit and healthy. Why did you bring him in?"

"He's been shaking his head a lot and scratching at his ears," I said.

She lifted one of the dog's floppy ears, stuck a scope into it, and peered in. Then she laughed.

"What is it?" I asked.

She smiled. "Swimmer's ear."

....

"Uh-oh," said Josh. "Riley's been digging holes again."

"How do you know?" I asked him from my seat on the couch where I was peacefully knitting.

"Look," he said, pointing to the dog who was standing at the back deck door covered in mud from the bottom of his dirty paws to the top of his head. Apparently not only had he dug some holes, he'd also rolled, bowled, and trolled through the holes like an oversized mole jacked up on Red Bull.

Yes, they are mostly lovable, but dogs, like people, have all kinds of annoying habits that can make you wish for a fake goldfish instead.

There are some dogs that are barkers and some dogs that are diggers and some dogs that like to chew on non-food things. My friend Ed's dog, Sadie, was a chewer. In addition to socks, she chewed on the moldings in their house, the linoleum floor, and the entire arm off a new sofa. Riley was a chewer and a digger. Given the chance, he'd dig a hole anywhere a hole could be dug, which was not such a big deal when the backyard was covered in snow, but was a landscaping nightmare when spring rolled around.

The issue was actually two-fold. When Riley dug a hole, not only were we left with an unattractive and potentially hazardous crater in the yard, but we were also left with an unattractive and definitively disgusting dog to bathe. Typically, it was up to Joel to find a way to fill the hole, and also typically it was up to me to bathe the dog. I think I got the shorter end of the stick. When I bathed the dog, I ended up having to clean the dog, the bathroom, and myself. So, while Joel got to throw down a piece of sod, I won the trifecta of dogmageddon. Not such a good deal.

I knew it was unlikely that we were going to be able to train the dog to stop digging, but I thought, at the very least, we should do something to even up the post-digging assignments.

As Joel walked into the room, I pointed to the dog on the deck.

"Ugh, not again," he groaned. "Let me go find the hole and fill it while you get a bath going."

"Not so fast, garden-boy," I retorted. "I think we need a new arrangement."

"What'ya mean?" he asked.

"I think I have the nastier job and we need a new deal," I replied. I thought for a minute. Then I said, "If the dog just digs an empty hole, you wash him. But if he actually digs up something, I'll do the dirty deed."

Since the dog had a 50/50 track record of digging stuff up, I thought this was a pretty good plan.

Joel thought this over and agreed. Then he went outside to find out who won the dirty dog bath lottery.

He came back a few moments later.

"Looks like you get to wash the dog," he grinned.

"What did he dig up?" I asked.

He held up a square of something suspiciously recognizable.

"A washcloth."

....

After the last round of dog-induced carpet cleaning, Emily came into the kitchen where I was cooking, appearing concerned.

"Mom, Riley is doing this weird thing," she announced somewhat urgently.

"Where?"

"In the family room."

"Naturally," I said.

I came around the corner of the kitchen in time to see the dog do this strange and completely revolting butt skooch across our rug.

"Aaaack!" I yelled. A proper response, I thought, to the sight of my dog using his rear end as a vacuum cleaner across the rug.

"No, no, no!" I barked at the dog, shooing him off the rug. He gave me a look as if to say, "What? Isn't this exactly what your spanking-clean rug is for?"

The dog skulked off, I assumed to go find another, less public rug to use to scratch his itch. Although I knew it came with the territory of owning a dog, I was still always surprised/horrified/revolted when my dog came up with a new and interesting way to violate our decor. While I had to give him points for creativity, I hesitated to buy anything of any value knowing the dog would find a way to desecrate or destroy it. Not coincidentally, it was the same philosophy I applied to the kids. But with the kids, if I told them not to skooch on the rug, at least they listened. The dog, not so much.

I picked up the phone and called the vet to make an appointment for the dog to get him checked out.

"He probably just needs to get his anal glands expressed," she said. "Usually that happens naturally when they pass a stool, but sometimes they need a little help."

"Okay, I'm not sure what you mean," I said. "But I really don't think I want to know because I'm betting that anything that involves expressing an anal gland is not going to be something I want to be a part of."

"You can bring him in and we'll do it," she said.

"I'm sure that will make your day," I replied.

When I got off the phone with Dr. Benson, I called the carpet cleaners to make an appointment to get the family room rug sandblasted again.

"Hi, this is Tracy Beckerman," I said to the carpet cleaning representative. "I'd like to make an appointment to get an area rug cleaned."

"Is this for a regular cleaning or has the rug been contaminated in some way?" she asked.

I snorted. "Oh, it's been contaminated, all right."

"Dirt, drink, or dog?" she asked.

"Dog," I responded.

"Front end or back end?" she inquired.

"Back end!" I said.

"Squat or skooch?"

"Skooch," I said.

"Okay, you will need our Defcon Four Decontamination Deal," she said. "That is a deep carpet cleaning combined with a special doggie butt skooching deterrent ingredient."

"That sounds perfect," I said.

"It comes with a one-year warranty against future skooching but does not protect against other doggie rug damage including muddy paws, nighttime garbage raids, rolling in dead things outside, toilet paper shredding, and other such canine-related atrocities."

"Got it," I said, giving the dog a death stare as he neared the rug again.

"Do you have other pets?" she asked.

"Yes. We have a lizard and a chinchilla."

"That's great! We are running a three-pet special!" she said excitedly. "For ten dollars more you get our patented Three Pet Protection Treatment and our Three Pet Guarantee."

"How does that work?" I asked.

"If all three pets contaminate the rug at the same time, we will come clean your carpet for free *and* take your pets away."

I glanced into the family room in time to see the kids trying to get the dog to do the "butt trick" again.

"Can you take the kids, too?" I wondered.

"Absolutely," she said.

"Deal!"

....

Over the years, scientists have discovered some universal truths: There are laws of physics, laws of gravity, laws of time and space.

I, Tracy Beckerman, have discovered yet another law . . . the law of dog puke. It goes like this: If you have one carpeted room or one good rug in your house, only one — that is the spot where your dog will throw up. Every time.

There is actually a scientific formula for this: $1 \times dog + rug = vomit$.

I don't know why this is true, but it is. In double-blind vomit tests, twenty out of twenty times Riley threw up, he did it on the rug.

In case we weren't one hundred percent absolutely sure of this fact, he did it again to prove the point on the brand new rug we had just bought to replace the other one that was so gross from all the other times he threw up on it.

When we picked out this rug we thought we were being really smart. We actually bought a dog vomit-colored rug. This helped enormously with the problem of discoloration, but did nothing for the smell.

It is worth mentioning that our house is eighty-five percent hard-wood floors. We have exactly three area rugs and they are mostly covered by furniture. A dog has to *really* go out of his way to dese-crate the area rugs in the house.

And yet, the dog, who weighed eighty-five pounds and was such a klutz he tripped going up the stairs, managed to tiptoe around the furniture every time he was sick to barf on the small square footage of carpet that was available. I would have given him high marks for agility had the result not been so stinkifying.

I should mention that in none of these instances was the dog really sick. Almost every time this happened, it was because he ate too fast or ate something bad or just felt like it. My kids are the same way. In the grand scheme of sick kids, you've got your pukers and your non-pukers. My kids are pukers. One time, Josh told his first-grade teacher he wasn't feeling well and when she didn't believe him and told him to sit down until the end of class, he puked on her shoes. He puked in the car, puked in his bed, and puked on the floor. He never made it to the toilet, which was the one place I wouldn't mind if he puked. Unfortunately, when the dog puked, the smell of it was so bad that it sometimes made the kids puke and this is primarily the reason I decided not to have any more dogs or kids.

With my miracle dog offense cleaning spray in hand, I man-aged to clean up the physical evidence of the doggie deed, but still, the smell lingered on. I threw open all the windows and doors and sprayed lemon-scented Super Dog Vomit Smell Be Gone air freshener all around the house until it was forty-two degrees in the house and smelled like a citrus grove. But as soon as the doors were closed and the lemons wafted away, there it was again.

Which led me to postulate a tandem scientific theory:

$1 \times$ dog vomit + rug = 1 year of your house smelling disgusting.

In the scheme of things, I suppose it could be worse . . .

At least we don't have to wall-to-wall carpeting.

....

Another birthday came around for Riley and we celebrated four years of him in our family with a peanut butter and kibble cake and some new stuffed toys. With the exception of my birthday in December, all our family birthdays and occasions fell during the summer, so it seemed apropos that Riley would also be a summer baby. Josh was in June. Joel and Emily were in July. Our anniversary was also in July, and Riley's birthday was in August. By the time we got to the dog's birthday, we were so birthday'd out that we were happy enough to let him have his own cake and eat it, too. Four years is not a monumental birthday for a dog, although technically, in dog years, he was now a young man. We did notice, however, that he had lost some of his puppy craziness and seemed to be moving away from both his sock fetish and his taste for grubs.

As Riley got older, so did the kids, and now that he was eleven, Josh was spending more time away from the house with his friends after school. Occasionally they would all gather at our house and take Riley out with them when they rode their skateboards, letting the dog pull them like he was a sled dog racing in the Iditarod. More than once Riley would get suddenly distracted by a squirrel, and then the unfortunate rider he was pulling would get yanked off his board and dragged into the street suffering some kind of street burn/squirrel-induced injury. Although I suggested to Josh and his friends that maybe this was not the best activity for either them or the dog, they persisted, and so I got to be an expert at cleaning up elbows and knees that had been skinned as a result of this game.

Even with this attention, Josh was out a lot and I noticed that Riley missed him. I knew this was only going to be more of an issue going forward, so I spent more time walking him and playing with him and encouraged Emily to do the same.

"Why don't you invite some friends over to play with Riley?" I said one day.

"Ah-ah," she said, shaking her head. "He smells bad."

I shoved my nose into the dog's neck and sniffed.

"I guess he could use a grooming."

"He doesn't need a grooming," she said. "He needs to be fumigated."

Fumigate was one of Emily's new favorite words. She also liked *voracious* and *preposterous* and tried to use them in a sentence whenever she could.

"It's because he eats all that dead stuff outside," she said, echoing what she'd heard me say. "He does that because he has a *voracious* appetite."

I smiled to myself. I had no idea where she got these from, but she was a voracious reader so it wouldn't be preposterous to think she picked them up from the books she read.

She quickly disappeared to play video games and I sniffed in the dog's general direction again to see if he was really all that bad. I wouldn't say that I'm nose blind to the smell of my dog, but I think, typically, I don't realize he needs a bath until the Board of Health shows up and condemns the dog, his bed, and our house.

Joel will usually smell him before I do. Maybe it's because he's out of the house all day and when he walks in the door, the smell hits him like a baseball bat to the face.

"Oh wow, the dog!" he said when he got home one night, putting his hand over his nose. "Don't you smell that?"

"Maybe a little," I admitted.

"When was the last time he had a bath?" he asked.

"Um, what year is it?"

Once Joel pointed out that our home was starting to smell like a decaying swamp, I realized the time had come to de-stinkify him (the dog, not my husband) before the government was called in to set up a hot zone around the perimeter of our house. I called to make an appointment with a new groomer I'd heard good things about. But they were booked solid by other people who no doubt had their own decaying swamp dogs.

I figured waiting a few days wouldn't make a huge difference since the Air Quality Index in the house was already at hazardous levels. I made the first available appointment and then sprayed the dog with air freshener for a couple of days until they could get him in.

The first hint that the new groomer's might not be the right place for us was in the waiting room. The space was wallpapered in a pink and green print with little French Bulldogs on it, and there were fuchsia-colored beanbag dog beds in the shapes of dog bones spread around the room for the dogs to recline on until their appointments. A bowl of free-range ostrich bites was on the counter, complimentary for all the pampered pups in the room who preferred their ostriches organic.

I looked at my dog, who seemed as stunned as I by the opulence. Apparently, the clientele here was used to a certain level of comfort and cuisine. Then there was my dog. He liked to sleep on bricks and eat dirt.

We waited for a short time until it was our turn.

"Riley Beckerman," a voice rang out.

We approached the counter.

"Are you getting the full-service grooming today?" asked the technician.

Not knowing what, exactly, the full-service was, I figured it probably included a wash, vacuum, and undercarriage spray, like we got for the car. So, I nodded yes.

"Would you like a rose, eucalyptus, or lemon-scented spa bath for Riley?" she continued.

I raised my eyebrows and glanced down at my dog. He had his head between his legs and was busy taking care of his own personal hygiene.

"Um, just regular clean dog scent, if you have it," I replied.

"We can do a plain cut or a cut, color, and curl," she said. "It's very popular with the poodles!"

"Just a plain cut, please."

"We can offer him a special non-GMO beverage and a light snack between procedures, if you'd like."

I looked at the dog again. He was chewing on his foot.

"That's okay. Just some water for him will do."

"Sparkling or tap?" she said.

This was better service than I got at my favorite restaurant, and I wasn't even expected to leave a tip. At least I didn't think I was.

"Tap is fine," I said.

"Okey dokey," she said cheerfully. "We do ask you to pay in advance. That will be one hundred and seventy-five dollars."

"*What?*" I screeched. "And that's without all the extra stuff?"

She nodded.

"Here," I said handing her the dog's leash. "You keep the dirty dog. I'm going to go out and adopt a clean one."

....

Midway through the summer, Riley decided to boycott his food. One day he just made up his mind that he'd had enough of the kibble, sniffed the bowl, and pushed it away with his nose, which was alarming since this was an animal that routinely ate anything and everything he found in the backyard, most of which did not even belong in the "food" category. Maybe compared to dirt, the kibble seemed bland. But after nearly four years, I had to wonder why he'd suddenly developed a sophisticated palate.

Being the dutiful pet owner that I am, I naturally consulted the veterinarian first to make sure there was no physical reason the dog wasn't eating. She assured me he was fine.

"So, how come he has become a picky eater?" I wondered.

"Do you ever feed him table scraps?" she asked.

"Never," I said haughtily. "Not counting the food that happens to land on the floor by mistake."

"Such as . . . "

"Steak, lasagna, the occasional tater tot that flies off the fork," I said.

"If you had a choice between tater tots and kibble, what would you pick?" she asked.

"I see your point," I said.

Since I was not prepared to whip up a gourmet meal for the dog each night, I decided we needed to get him to go back to his kibble-eating ways. I thought if I mixed in some treats to make the meal more appetizing, it might help with his pickiness.

So, first I added some peanut butter.

He licked the peanut butter off the kibble and left the rest.

Then I sprinkled some shredded cheese on the kibble.

He flipped the bowl over and then ate the shredded cheese off the floor.

Finally, I laid out a trail of tater tots to his food bowl and buried a few more tots at the bottom of the bowl. He ate the tots, ignored the kibble, and then went outside and ate some more grubs. I was worried that the dog was never going to eat dog food again. But I was more worried that the People for the Ethical Treatment of Grubs were going to come after me.

"Stop giving him people food," said the vet. "When he gets hungry enough, he'll eat the kibble."

"Why would he eat the kibble when there is a veritable buffet of grubs and deer poop outside?" I wondered.

"I see your point," she said.

We finally decided to change his kibble. I guess after nearly four years, I would be kind of sick of salmon and sweet potato, too.

After some deliberation, we switched him over to a hypoaller-genic lamb kibble. He warily approached the bowl, sniffed the food, and then devoured it. For an entire week, he happily ate his new food. Then one day I let him outside and watched in dismay as he sucked down a couple of grubs.

"I don't get it," I said to Dr. Benson. "He likes the new kibble. So why is he still eating grubs?"

"Oh. Well you know what they say about grubs," she said.

"No. What?"

"Tastes like chicken."

....

When the time came to close the pool for the season, the saddest person in the family was not me or Joel or either of the kids. It was the dog. He went into a real funk, and after working so hard to get his weight down we noticed that Riley had started to get a little rounder again. Without the swimming, he wasn't getting much exercise and it had begun to show.

"I caught the dog looking at himself in the full-length mirror today," I said to my husband. "I think he's feeling a little self-conscious about his thighs. And he's worried about putting on weight over the holidays."

"The dog is worried?" my husband asked.

"Yes, he noticed that he's put a few pounds on since Labor Day and he wants to make sure he doesn't get any heavier."

"The dog said that?" Joel said.

"He did," I assured him.

It was true that the dog *had* put on a little weight. But he wasn't the only one. After a summer of barbecue and birthday cakes, I was having trouble fitting into my skinny jeans. Now, with Halloween and then Thanksgiving looming, I needed to stop and face the music or I'd end up looking as round as the holiday turkey.

I've heard that you're more likely to succeed on a food and exercise plan if you do it with a friend, so I decided to enlist the help of a partner. I wanted someone who would go along with whatever exercise I decided to do, who wouldn't scold me if I cheated on my diet, and would be a willing participant in any harebrained get-thin-quick scheme I came up with.

So, I drafted the dog.

"Riley needs to lose a few pounds again," I said to Dr. Benson at our next visit. "What do you recommend?"

"You can cut down on his food intake," she suggested.

"Oh, but then won't we, I mean, he, be hungry?"

"He's a dog. He's always hungry," she said.

"Yes," I sighed. "We are. I mean, he is."

She looked at me and raised an eyebrow.

"Or we could switch him to a lower-calorie kibble and you can supplement with carrots and string beans."

"That might work," I replied. "I like carrots. I mean, the dog likes carrots."

Riley thumped his tail. Dr. Benson gave me the side-eye.

"You know, a lot of times dogs gain weight because of too much snacking. Do you think that might be the problem here?" she asked.

"Definitely," I replied.

"If you cut down on the snacks, you probably wouldn't need to change the meals."

"Really? You think so?" I felt myself growing excited.

"Yes. Stop snacking and get more exercise."

"I can do that!" I exclaimed. "I mean, I can help Riley with that."

She and I lifted the dog off the examination table and he thanked her by licking the entirety of her face. I don't think it was because he liked her. I think he was just hungry.

"I'm sure with a few small changes, Riley will drop the weight pretty quickly," she said and winked at me.

"Thanks so much," I said to her as I put the dog's leash back on him. "I'm sure the dog appreciates your advice. Do you have any other suggestions?"

"Yes," she said. "Don't keep any leftover Halloween candy."

....

"I had a talk with Riley and he understands his behavior has not been great of late and he'd like to make some changes," I said to Joel. We were sitting up in bed looking at both of our laptops while the dog slept peacefully on the floor.

"Really?"

"Yes, as he's gotten older, he's become very self-aware."

Joel closed the computer and eyed me suspiciously. "The dog told you this?"

"Well, not exactly," I admitted. "But I felt his remorse, so I helped him write up a list of ways he can improve upon his dogginess in the coming year."

Truth be told, Riley did not need to do much to be a better dog. He was a great fetch dog (even when he wouldn't give back the things he fetched), a polite member of the family (even when he passed gas and tried to blame it on someone else), and an incredibly affection-ate animal (even when he tried to French kiss the mailman). I really didn't think he needed to improve upon his dog skills. However, as a retriever, he set a high bar for himself and I could sense that he wanted to set some personal goals . . . and who am I to get in the way of his self-improvement ambitions?

I got down on the floor to give the dog moral support while I read from the list. "Number one: Riley endeavors to break his underwear and sock chewing habit, or at least cut it down to one pair of socks a day."

Riley nodded in agreement. My husband also approved.

"Number two: Riley promises to dig fewer holes out back so our backyard will no longer resemble the surface of the moon."

Riley crossed his paws. I wasn't sure he was a hundred percent behind that resolution.

"Number three: Riley resolves not to pee in the house when a service technician comes to repair something," I continued.

"*Anywhere* in the house?" Joel wondered.

"He can't promise the floor but he guarantees the family room rug."

Riley and my husband exchanged conciliatory glances.

"Number four: Riley agrees not to steal any food off the kitchen counter, as long as it's not steak, chicken, eggs, tuna fish, or peanut butter."

Joel looked at me skeptically. "So, basically he's agreeing not to steal vegetables off the counter?"

"Take it or leave it," I said.

He rolled his eyes. Riley quietly spiked the imaginary football.

"Okay, last one," I added. "Number five: Riley resolves not to bark at invisible intruders, phantom cars, and imaginary squirrels in the middle of the night when we are sleeping."

"I love that resolution," my husband said.

". . . but he asks that in return, you don't keep him up with your snoring."

Joel narrowed his eyes at me. "The dog said that?"

I nodded.

"Okay," he said. "I'll try to do that as long as he doesn't hog the bathroom in the mornings."

I squinted back at him. "Riley doesn't use the bathroom."

". . . And I don't snore," my husband retorted.

We glared at each other for a moment. "Tell you what," I said. "Riley won't hog the bathroom if you won't snore, and he won't chew up your underwear."

Riley licked himself, and Joel pecked me on the cheek.

"Deal," he said. "Now, when can we get the kids to work on their lists?"

PART TWO

ONE FISH, TWO FISH, DEAD FISH, BLUE FISH

The problem with getting several pets is that your children then have this expectation that more will follow. I made the same mistake the first time I gave Josh french fries. Once he tasted those, there was no turning back to apple slices: I had opened the door to junk food. Similarly, once we had the dog, the Beckerman Zoo was open for business.

Such was the case when Josh was twelve and arrived home from our local street fair with a live prize in a plastic baggie.

"I won him," Josh said gleefully, holding up the baggie with a pathetic-looking goldfish in it.

"What did the loser get?" I asked, peering at the sad specimen of a fish.

Josh ignored me. "His name is Vladimir," he said adoringly.

"It seems like a strong name," I said. "Especially if you're an impaler."

"Can we keep him?" said Josh.

I sighed. We'd been down this trout stream before. We get a fish. We get the fish stuff. A week later, the fish is doing the backstroke and we're hovering over the toilet giving the fish last rites and preparing for a burial at sea.

"You know those things never last," I warned him.

"No, Vladimir is hearty," he protested. "He'll live to be a hundred. Besides, you should think of him as a rescue fish. We're just doing our part to make sure one more goldfish doesn't go through life without a forever home."

I shook my head. "Josh, you already have a pet. Two pets, actually. And Emily has a pet. Although technically they are all my pets because I feed them and clean up after them."

"I feed Einstein," he said.

"You throw crickets in the tank after I buy them and keep them alive. But you always miss a few and then they get loose in the house and go in the vents and at four in the morning it sounds like we are camping in the Appalachian Mountains. Besides, I really don't want to add Head Fish Keeper and Future Fish Funeral Director to my resumé."

"Ten bucks he's sushi by Thursday," said Emily, who was hovering nearby.

I knew Josh had brought her along to throw him her support, but at ten years old, she had bigger fish to fry. In the grand scheme of things, it was more satisfying to throw her brother to the sharks than to help him get what he wanted. I was pretty sure money had exchanged hands in this deal and he would be coming back to her to demand a refund.

"I'm going to have to check with Dad," I said. "But I'm not sure what you should do with Vlad in the meantime. I guess we can foster him in our old tank. But don't get too attached," I warned him.

"How could you get attached to a stupid fish?" asked Emily.

"Hey Em, let's not make fun of Josh for caring about animals."

"Okay, Steve Irwin," said Emily. "I'm sorry I made fun of you. I'm sure Vlad will be a strong fish and will live a long, healthy life until he gets tail rot and dies."

I shook my head and reminded myself that one day they would be the best of friends. If they survived adolescence together.

Ultimately, I acquiesced, not because I expected that Vladimir would surprise us with his longevity or because I thought caring for a fish would teach my kids some responsibility. It hadn't worked with our dog, lizard, or chinchilla, so I didn't think it would work with Vladimir the Wonder Fish, either.

No, I caved because we still had a fish tank and some food leftover from the last short-term aquatic resident, named Wolfgang Amadeus Beckerman, who was not a famous music composer, but rather, at the end, a formidable decomposer. Besides, the fair was over, so now there was no giving Vlad back. We were on the hook, so to speak, and there was no way to worm out of it. From past experience, though, I knew it would only last a week at most.

"Okay, fine," I said. "He can stay. But you feed him. You change the water, if he lives that long, and if at any point I find a sorry-looking goldfish in my sink or bathtub, you'll both be in hot water."

So, now we had another addition to the Beckerman Zoo. I did the math and realized that before Vlad, the humans in the house had the advantage — there were four of us to three of them. But now the teams were tied, which meant any day the animals could rise up and overthrow the ruling class and then it would be all kibble, all the time. Of course, I'm not convinced the fish could instigate an uprising, but the lizard would. Since I was fairly certain that Vlad was not going to be around long enough to tilt the balance of power anyway, I didn't give it too much thought.

Josh, however, was sure that Vlad was going to follow him to the retirement community. The next day he went to the pet store and used his allowance money to buy some pebbles, plants, and other must-have fish tank accessories for the fashionable goldfish. Vladimir was now one cool sea dude. He was the Big Kahuna. The Kingfish. Goldy Dick.

"You're wasting your money," I said to Josh.

"He'll outlive us all," he responded.

I waited a day. A week. Two weeks. But shockingly, Vlad shouldered on, or rather, floated and swam on. I surrendered.

"I guess he's staying," I said reluctantly. "Ack, four pets! I can't handle it."

My son smiled. "Come on, Mom. Let's get your mind off it. Wanna play cards?"

"Sure. What game?" I asked.

He smirked. "How about Go Fish?"

....

There's a saying that goes, "The first to come is the last to leave." In the case of our fish, Vlad was the last to come and the first to leave.

"Mom, come here," Josh called to me from across the house.

"What?" I yelled back. We had just returned from a weekend at the beach and I was trying to sort out the dirty clothes from the truly disgusting wet and sandy dirty clothes that threatened to walk away on their own if I didn't catch them and herd them into the washing machine.

"It's Vlad," he yelled again. "He's not swimming." *Not swimming* could be merely resting, or perhaps just deep in thought. Unfortunately, when I peered into the tank, it was immediately clear that *not swimming* was *not alive*.

"I'm really sorry, kiddo." I said putting my hand on his shoulder. "It looks like Vlad has gone to that great big fishbowl in the sky."

"You mean he's dead?" he asked.

We both looked at the decomposing fish lying on the bottom of the tank. He was either dead or doing yoga. I put my money on dead.

"'Fraid so," I said sympathetically.

"He had a really long life for a carnival fish, though," I assured him. "He lived for ten months. That's like one hundred in goldfish years."

"What should we do?" he asked. "Should we bury him?"

"Um, maybe not such a good idea," I said, recalling how Riley had discovered the previous owner's dead hamster cemetery in the back of the yard and eaten all the residents.

"How about we have a funeral in the bathroom?" I suggested.

"You mean flush him down the toilet?"

"I prefer to think of it as a burial at sea," I said.

I sent Josh off to work on an appropriate eulogy and then I informed the rest of the family of the sad news.

"Well, that's one less animal we have to feed," said Joel.

"I'm glad it wasn't my pet," said Emily.

I shook my head at the two of them. "Your sympathy overwhelms me. Come on, we're going to have a funeral."

"For a fish?" asked Joel.

"Glad it wasn't my pet," Emily repeated.

"Can't we just feed him to the dog?" asked Joel.

I whacked him. "Ssh! Vlad was a part of the family and I think we should give him a proper send-off for Josh, okay?"

Admittedly, Josh was not that broken up over the demise of his pet fish. However, being the touchy-feely mom that I am, I thought I should give him the opportunity to express his feelings and mourn his loss, miniscule as it might have been.

As the family assembled in the bathroom, we stood shoulder to shoulder around the toilet bowl while Joel held the dead fish out in the dead fish net.

"We are here today to say goodbye to Vladimir, the goldfish,"

Josh said. "He was a loyal companion and had a great sense of humor — you know, for a fish." We all nodded in agreement. "He will be missed."

I sniffled. My husband looked at my son, who gave him the nod. And then Vlad took his final swim.

"Okay?" I asked.

"Yeah," said Josh solemnly.

"How about dinner?" asked Joel.

Josh brightened. "Can we get sushi?"

....

Not long after we flushed our dead goldfish down the toilet, the kids were bucking for a replacement.

"Let's get another goldfish," said Josh. "No, let's get two, so they're not lonely."

"How could it be lonely? It will have a dog, chinchilla, and lizard to keep it company," I said.

"So then it's okay if we get another fish?" he asked.

"I didn't say that!" I yelled.

I wasn't surprised that they were asking for a new pet. I was just surprised that it had taken as long as it did, and at least they weren't looking for a furry upgrade. I figured it was just a matter of time before they figured out that the fish tank could also hold a small snake, rodent, or crustacean. But I certainly was not about to point that out to them. In the meantime, I relocated the empty fish tank to the basement so no one would have any visual reminders of its emptiness.

Unfortunately, the plan backfired. Without the fish tank around, they gave up on the idea of a small animal and started negotiating for a larger one.

"Could we get a llama?" Emily asked again as she watched a documentary about alpacas on TV.

"Seriously Em, the llama thing again? I already told you we're not zoned for large South American animals that spit."

"Henry is from South America," Josh argued.

"Henry is from the pet store, and he is a *small* South American animal," I said.

"But llamas are really cool," Emily continued. "And I could ride it to school so you wouldn't have to drive me, and you could make us sweaters from the wool."

I snickered. Although I could knit, I was pretty sure I had no knowledge of how to shear a llama or spin wool into yarn. But that was so beside the point.

"What would you do with the llama once you got to school?" I asked her.

"Lock it to the bike rack," she answered logically.

"What if someone stole it?"

"Come on, Mom. I think it would be pretty easy to find a stolen llama," she said matter of factly. "They're not exactly easy to hide."

"No llamas."

"How about a pot-bellied pig?" Josh suggested. "They are extremely smart."

"No pigs."

"But it can eat all our garbage," he countered.

"We already have a dog that does that," I said.

"How about a scorpion? Or a boa constrictor?" he asked gleefully.

"No! I draw the line at pets that can poison or swallow you." I decided I'd better quickly end this conversation before someone suggested anything else that was either big enough to ride on or deadly enough to be featured on the Discovery Channel.

"We are not getting another pet!" I announced. "We have three pets and we do not need a fourth. The zoo is closed."

Before someone could suggest a pet rock, the phone rang.

"Hey, hey, it's Uncle Day!" said my brother. He lived way up in the Malibu mountains where they had wild cougars and coyotes running amok, among other animals that could kill or maim you. I always thought it was interesting that he made fun of me for spending time in New York City, which he thought was the most dangerous place in the country, while he lived in a place with wild-fires, mudslides, earthquakes, and sinkholes, as well as wild animals and the equally frightening self-involved celebrities. I put him on speakerphone so the kids could talk, too.

"Hey Uncle Day!" they both yelled.

"Sorry to hear about your goldfish," he said.

"It's okay," they said in unison.

"So, guess what?" he said. "We found a tarantula outside our front door. Do you guys need a new pet to replace the goldfish?"

I slammed the phone down on the counter. The kids looked at me questioningly. I shrugged.

"Wrong number."

....

After Vlad passed, a friend gifted us three goldfish to make up for the loss.

We are no longer friends.

The fish, naturally, were nonrefundable, so we dug out the old fish tank again, set it up, and named the little fishies Larry, Moe, and Curly, after the Three Stooges, although I was probably the biggest stooge for keeping more goldfish. The three fishies all seemed to be getting on swimmingly. Then Joel went out of town on business.

As I mentioned before, whenever Joel leaves town, one of three things invariably happen: One of the kids get sick, something in the house breaks, or one of the pets dies.

So, what are the chances that when he went away one week, all three of these things would happen at the same time?

"Mom, I have a stomachache, the downstairs toilet's not flushing, and one of the fish is swimming upside down," said Josh as he stood in front of me in his pajamas one morning before school. I could see his face was flushed with a fever and I knew immediately that he would not be going to school that day.

I looked at him and shook my head in disbelief.

"Really? All three?"

He nodded and then covered his mouth and ran to the bathroom.

"No!! Puke in the upstairs toilet!!" I yelled after him. "The downstairs toilet isn't flushing."

Yeah, I'm a shoo-in for Mom of the Year.

While Josh dealt with either a stomach virus or the enchilada he ate with his friends the day before, I went into the kitchen to suss out the fish situation.

I spotted Larry and Moe right away doing the happy "we're gonna get fed" dance they always do when they see me approach the fish tank in the morning. Then I noticed Curly. He was listlessly doing the sidestroke in a way I had seen many fish before him do right before they went to that great fishbowl in the sky . . . or that small toilet bowl in the bathroom, as the case may be.

Thinking about my mass of good fortune that morning, I took heart. I was confident that Josh had a twenty-four-hour bug and would be better in a day or so. I had a good feeling that I could get the toilet fixed relatively quickly. However, looking at Curly, I was pretty sure that he was going to glub his last glub before the day was over.

The bad news, of course, was not that Curly was about to be sleeping with the fishes, as they say. The bad news was that the fish was about to go belly up while Josh was at home, which would make it exceedingly difficult to ditch the dead fish, run out and buy a look-alike fish, and make the swap without being detected. Yes, even though the kids were ten and twelve and I knew they could handle an SFD (Sudden Fish Death), I still went to the pet store when a fish died and the kids weren't home to buy a look-alike fish so I wouldn't be accused of being the one who caused the fish to die. I was a lot of things, but fish murderer wasn't one of them, and I needed to maintain my good fish-keeper reputation.

Abandoning the dying fish, I checked on Josh, set him up with some saltines and ginger ale, and sent him back to bed. Then I checked in on the toilet. It was filled to the rim with water and paper and did not respond to my best efforts to plunge it. If Joel had been in town, I would have hung a "do not use" sign on the door and left the toilet alone until he got home. But since he was not home, I did the next best thing. I hung a "do not use" sign on the door and called a plumber.

"It's just really badly clogged," the plumber said as he snaked out the inner plumbing of the toilet. "It's a pretty old toilet. You shouldn't put anything in there except toilet paper."

I thought for a minute. "How about something really small?" I asked.

"How small?"

I glanced at the fish tank in the kitchen. Then held up my thumb and forefinger about an inch apart.

"Yay big."

....

The day started innocently enough. I made the rounds feeding all the pets as I did every morning. I fed the fish, the dog, and the chinchilla. I let the dog out. I let the dog in. I drove the kids to school, stopped at the pet shop to pick up more crickets for the lizard, and then I came home. And that is when I saw it: The door to the chinchilla cage was open and the chinchilla was gone.

Henry the amazing disappearing chinchilla had escaped once

again. I considered changing his name to Harry Houdini instead, but decided against it because Houdini died at a relatively young age and if that happened to Henry, I'd have a much bigger problem on my hands than a missing chinchilla.

Losing the chinchilla was indeed a problem, as we had learned once before. But losing a chinchilla the day before you leave for vacation was more than a problem. It was a disaster.

Scanning the crime scene, I quickly noted that Henry was nowhere in sight. However, since Henry left a disgusting path of poops behind him, it was easy to follow his trail. I started at the chinchilla's cage and like Lewis and Clark before me, followed the trail.

Without needing to use too many of my navigation skills, I saw that Henry had left the cage and meandered into the kitchen. Next, he sashayed through the dining room and on into the bathroom, where he decided to investigate the inside of the bathtub.

Did I mention that chinchillas can jump?

Apparently, he jumped into the bathtub, and then jumped out of the bathtub, hopped up onto the toilet seat, which fortunately was closed, back onto the floor, out of the bathroom, into the hall, down the hall, into the office, out of the office, back into the hall, down the hall, and to the bottom of the stairs.

This is when the trail ran cold.

While chinchillas can jump, I was pretty confident that they could not do a whole flight of stairs, so I retraced the poop trail and found . . . nothing.

Concerned that I still had a bunch of things to do on my vacation to-do list before we left, I decided to take a break from the chinchilla hunt and hope that Henry would emerge from his hiding place before it was time to go.

Taking one last look around, I grabbed the bag of crickets I had bought that morning and went upstairs to feed the last pet, Josh's lizard. Of course, in the space of five minutes I had totally forgotten all about the lost chinchilla and therefore was completely stunned when Henry suddenly darted out from under Josh's bed, scaring me mid-cricket-feeding.

In my shock at seeing the fleeing chinchilla, I gasped, flung the bag, and sent sixty crickets ricocheting off Josh's bedroom wall.

Some of the crickets must have been boomerang crickets because a few of them bounced off the wall and landed back on me, with one of them slipping right down the front of my shirt. Since I am not a big fan of insecty-things, I screamed and writhed frantically to rid myself of the crickets. Unfortunately, while doing so, I somehow smacked my chin on the edge of my son's steel bed and chipped off a large piece of my lower front tooth.

Sitting on my son's bed with a chipped tooth, crickets hopping all over the place, and a freaked-out chinchilla, I decided that there was really just one thing I needed: a vacation.

....

Most people take vacations as a break from work, school, and laundry. Personally, I needed a vacation just from getting ready to go on vacation. The hardest part about going away was not the getting-everything-I-need part, or the packing-everything-up part, or holding the mail, stopping the newspapers, or getting my tooth fixed so I didn't look like a hockey goalie. No, for me, the biggest pain in the neck was finding someone to come in while we were away and feed Einstein.

Getting someone to take care of your furry animals is usually pretty easy because the pets are cute and cuddly. Finding someone to take care of your sometimes constipated, cold-blooded lizard that's the size of your arm and eats live insects is another story.

When I complained about this to my friends, they said, "Why

don't you just board him, like your dog?" That would be a good solution, if I were a weightlifter, because the lizard had grown so much we'd had to move him into a ninety-gallon tank, and I would hate to start my vacation with a herniated disc and a ruptured spleen. So then my friends said, "Why don't you just leave a ton of food in his tank?" This, too, would be a good solution, if the lizard wasn't a pig and wouldn't eat a week's worth of crickets in one fell swoop and then throw up, like my kids do when I give them a bag of candy and tell them to just have a few pieces.

It was one thing to be the mother of the kid with the lizard and have to scoop a dozen live crickets out of a container, into a plastic bag with vitamin powder, and then into the lizard tank. It was quite another to ask someone else to do it. I thought about paying the neighbor's kid to come over and do it, because I was fairly certain that a fourteen-year-old boy would have no problem handling a veritable plague of disgusting bugs. However, I was also fairly certain that for every cricket he caught, ten more would escape into the crevices of my home, only to reappear later on my face while I slept or in the bathroom when my mother visited or on the head of the third new cleaning lady I just hired who still didn't even know about the lizard.

We were still catching errant crickets from the last cricket jailbreak, so maybe the solution was to just let Einstein loose and let him feed off the fat of the land, so to speak. Plus, with the dog away, Einstein could patrol the house and keep intruders away. I know if I went to rob a house and a lizard the size of a Smart Car came around the corner hissing and blowing up his beard, I wouldn't stick around to find out if he only ate crickets.

However, if for some reason we were unable to locate him when we got home, I think it would be infinitely more shocking for my mother to be visiting and have a lizard appear in the bathroom rather than a little cricket.

But as we were approaching our vacation date, I thought to ask my responsible, college-aged babysitter if she would mind coming in to feed Einstein.

"No problem," she said.

So, I left her the key, the crickets, a wad of money, and some very explicit instructions.

I wouldn't say I spent the entire vacation worried about what was going on with Einstein in my absence, but I did have more than one passing thought that we might get home and find out that the crickets had all escaped and taken over the house, the neighborhood, and quite possibly the world.

I recalled the time that I got tired of going to the pet store once a week to get more crickets and thought I would be smart and order a box of five hundred live crickets delivered to our house. Yes, five hundred. I bought an extra-large plastic container for all of them, a ton of cricket food, and then congratulated myself on coming up with a way to make my hectic life simpler. When the box arrived, I regrettably missed the small circle on the side of the carton that said, "Open Here," and instead, enthusiastically ripped the top off the box, allowing five hundred cooped-up crickets to launch themselves out of the box, all over the floor, and into the house.

"Aaaaahhh," I yelled, as crickets flew into my face, my hair, at the dog.

"Aaaaahhh," yelled Emily, who had been watching the cricket unboxing. We both continued to scream and jumped onto kitchen chairs, which did nothing because the crickets were jumping into the air as well.

"We have to be brave and stop the crickets," I finally said to her. "I'm going in."

I jumped down off the chair and started scooping up crickets to get them back in the box. Emily jumped off the chair and started stomping on crickets. Riley did his part by eating crickets.

In the end, we probably only ended up recovering about twenty crickets, which left four hundred eighty crickets that made it into the air conditioning vents, and for a year it sounded like we were living in the marshes during cricket mating season.

"What if we get home and all the crickets escaped and the babysitter is missing and Einstein is dead?" I said to Joel as we sat on the beach on vacation, and I relived that horrible moment in my mind.

"If that happens, we'll get a new lizard, buy more crickets, and find a new babysitter," he replied.

Ten days later when our vacation was over, we arrived home and I immediately went to Josh's room. All the crickets were gone and the lizard looked fat and happy, or at least, fat and alive. I assumed this was because he had eaten the crickets, not the babysitter.

"Success," I said to Joel, gesturing to the tank as he walked into the room. But before he could congratulate me, we heard Emily scream from the floor below.

"Mom, come here quick! There's crickets in the bathroom!"

I looked at Joel and then picked up the phone.

"Who are you calling?" he asked.

"The babysitter," I said. "I just want to make sure she's alive."

....

"This is Rocky," said my dad, handing Emily his wriggling new Shetland Sheepdog puppy. Rocky was about ten weeks old and like all puppies, he was insanely cute. I have to admit, I was surprised my folks had a new dog. They were in their seventies and lived in a retirement community down in Florida. Most of the residents there were at the point in their lives where they were done with kids and dogs and were happy to just have grandchildren to spoil and give back to their parents when the kids started to scream. My folks liked to play golf and go out to eat and take road trips across Florida so they could come back every time and say how much nicer the beaches were on the East Coast than the West Coast. It seemed there was little room in their lives for a new puppy.

The dog was actually my dad's idea. He was the pet person in our family when I was growing up, so this was not totally out of character for him. He was the one who found stray kittens on the road when he was out running and would bring them home. He was also the one who announced one of the kittens was a female and named her Sadie, who, unfortunately, was stuck with that name even after the vet declared that Sadie was, in fact, a male. My dad picked out our first Golden Retriever, Honey, our second Golden, Fanny, our Yellow Lab, Sugar, and our Siberian Husky, Sasha. He got Sasha because all of his kids had brown eyes and he wanted an offspring with blue eyes, like him. Not that my dad was shallow or anything. Sasha, unfortunately, was not a good fit for our family. Siberian Huskies have an enormous amount of energy, which is what makes them great sled dogs. They also stay puppies, mentally, until well after they turn two years old, which means all that extra puppy energy hangs around for a long time and has to get funneled somewhere. In Sasha's case that meant eating the arm off our living room sofa, gnawing off a large corner of the oriental rug, and chewing up a third of the linoleum floor in the kitchen and all but one of the rattan kitchen chairs. At one point, my dad was on a work call and the dog would not stop howling, so he put Sasha in the bathroom for a moment to finish the call. In the space of three minutes Sasha ripped down the shower curtain, chewed up the toilet seat lid, and knocked down the bathroom door and split it in half. After that, Sasha was sent back to the breeders in the Great White North from whence he came to pull sleds and scare off hungry moose.

Naturally, Emily couldn't care less why my folks had a new dog and whether it was a good move for them. Josh thought the dog was cute, but he was more interested in hunting anoles around my parents' property than playing with Rocky. But Emily spent the entire three-day visit with the puppy and when we got home, I could see that she still had puppy love in her eyes. I knew it was just a matter of time before the begging began.

"I think Riley is lonely," she said, glancing at the dog who did not look very lonely at all, but rather, asleep. "We should get a puppy."

"Not on your life," I responded succinctly.

"Why?"

"Because we have one dog, a chinchilla, a bearded dragon, and two goldfish that I have to feed every day."

"I'll feed the puppy!"

"No puppy!" I shouted.

She pouted and stomped out of the room. I didn't care. If pouting and stomping actually worked, we would have had ten dogs, an Icelandic pony out back, his llama friend, and a dolphin in the pool.

I hoped that once we were home and back into our routine, she would forget about the cute puppy and I could go back to managing the rest of our menagerie in peace, or as close as you get to peace with four pets.

But this was not the case. Recently it seemed everyone in the world had a new puppy. Our next-door neighbors had adopted a floppy-eared German Shepherd rescue puppy. My friend Ed had a new Golden Retriever puppy. Even the school crossing guard had acquired a new puppy that he brought with him to work and wore on his chest in an infant carrier while he stopped traffic so the kids could cross the street. It seemed that every time we went out, there was puppy cuteness staring us in the face.

"Doesn't anyone neuter their dogs?" I demanded after we ran into yet another friend with an armful of puppy.

"Pleeeeeaaaaasssseee!" Emily begged when we got home. "Can we get a puppy?"

"No. Absolutely not," said I, the meanest puppy-depriving mother of all time.

"Why not?"

"You know why not," I said.

She stuck out her lower lip. Then she thought for a minute.

"Okay. How 'bout a kitten?"

"You know your brother and your dad are allergic to cats," I reminded her.

She stomped out of the room once again to show her displeasure. By this point I was immune to my children's desire for more animals, so I let the dog out and went back to making dinner. But no sooner had I put the pasta up to boil than I heard a tap at the back deck door. I looked over and saw the dog waiting patiently to be let back in.

"That was fast," I said to him. I looked down and on closer inspection, I noticed something in his mouth. Certain that it was either dead or about to be dead, I told him to lie down and then pried open his jaws so whatever it was would fall to the floor without me having to touch it. A moment later, there was a baby bunny on the floor. It appeared to be fine, if a little stunned, and I suspected Riley had "retrieved" it from a rabbit hole I had seen in the backyard.

As I was contemplating how to return it to its mother now that it had dog smell all over it, my daughter came bounding back into the room. She looked down at the floor where I was squatting and screamed.

"A bunny!" she crowed. "Riley brought us a baby bunny."

"He didn't bring it for us. He rabbit-napped it," I said.

"Hey Josh," she yelled, ignoring me. "We have a new pet. Riley brought us a baby bunny. Thank you, Riley." She said and hugged the dog around the neck. "You are a very good boy!"

Josh came running down the stairs, looked at the bunny, shrugged and left. Apparently, bunnies were okay. Tarantulas were better.

I shook my head. I was about to be in the doghouse again.

"We can't keep it, Em," I told her gently, stopping her as she bent down to pick up the bunny. "It's not a pet. It belongs outside and its mother is probably looking for it."

She thrust out her lower lip. "I can be its mother."

I put my arm around her. "How about you help me find a shoebox for it and then we can go outside and look for its home together, okay?"

She sighed deeply. "Okay."

Ten minutes later, flashlight in hand, we found the rabbit hole exactly where I thought it would be.

"We'll just leave the baby bunny right outside the hole so it doesn't bring the dog smell in. And then when the momma hears it, she'll come out and bring it in. And tomorrow I'll section off that part of the yard so Riley won't go near it again."

She nodded sadly.

When we got back in the house she brightened up almost immediately.

"We saved a bunny!" she said.

"Yes we did," I agreed.

" . . . And now that we know Riley gets along with rabbits, we can get another one!"

....

In the span of one week, I lost two fish and a coffee maker. I didn't think there was a relationship between the two, but I was pretty sad about all of them, nonetheless. First there was the untimely death of our fish Curly. Then suddenly Moe bit the dust. And finally, our coffee maker blew during its last brew. I waited the requisite two days of mourning, and then went out and bought more fish and a new coffee maker.

While Joel could understand the coffee maker purchase, he couldn't fathom why I would get more fish. We'd had a revolving door, or fish tank, as it were, of goldfish ever since Josh and Emily started bringing them home from the local street fairs. I lost count of the number of fish we'd had, and lost, because most came and went within twenty-four hours. The quick-turnaround fish barely got a eulogy on their final trip to Fish Heaven, or the toilet, as it was more commonly known in our house. Just a simple, "He was a good fish," and then a flush. I guess our hearts had been hardened by so many losses.

This being the case, everyone was certainly surprised when I arrived home with a new plastic bag filled with goldfish.

"Larry is lonely," I explained, gesturing to the lone fish in our tank. "He arrived in that tank with his brothers Curly and Moe and now he is the only one left."

"He's not lonely. He's a *fish*," Joel said.

"Look how listless he is," I said. "He's lonely."

"Yeah honey . . . I hate to break it to you, but that doesn't look like listless. That looks like tail rot. And that is how the other two fish looked before they bit the big one."

I shook my head in disagreement and plunked the bag of fish into the tank so the new fish could acclimate to the temperature of the new tank, and all the fish could get to know each other.

"Okay," sighed my husband, realizing that he was not going to win the fish wars. "What are we calling these new fish?"

"Larry."

"Which one is Larry?" he asked.

"They are all Larry," I said.

"Isn't the old one called Larry?" he wondered.

"Yes, the old one is Larry and the new ones are Larry. They are all Larry."

Joel stared at me with a look of sheer confusion on his face.

This is a common look for him when I do strange things, so I just waited.

"And you are naming them all Larry, why . . . ?"

I took a deep breath. "Honestly, I always have trouble telling the fish apart, so the next time one dies, I will be secure in the knowledge that the one that died is Larry."

Just as I finished my explanation, the kids arrived home from school.

"Hey look, Mom got some new fish!" Emily exclaimed.

" . . . And a new coffee maker," said Josh.

"Yeah," said my husband dryly. "Its name is Larry."

....

Although my family disagreed, I thought it was a brilliant move to name all the new goldfish Larry. Every morning I went downstairs and said "Hi Larry!" and all four fish felt personally greeted in one fell swoop. When it was time to feed the fish, I told everyone it was time to feed the Larrys, thus saving myself precious seconds that I otherwise would have spent listing four names. Had I been really smart, I would have named the dog, chinchilla, lizard, and both my kids Larry, too. I think Josh would have been fine with this, but I don't think Emily would have been too happy with me.

Things went along swimmingly with the four Larrys until one day the inevitable happened: One of the Larrys kicked the bucket.

"Oh no," I cried, when I went to feed the fish and saw the floater. "Larry died."

"Which one?" asked my husband.

"Larry."

"I know it was Larry. Which Larry?"

"The dead one."

"Which one is the dead one?"

"Larry."

"Which Larry??"

"The one that died."

"I think *I'm* going insane," he said. "Let's start over. You bought three fish from the fish store . . . "

"Yes."

"You named them all Larry . . . "

"Right."

"One died . . ."

"Sadly."

"Which one was it?"

"Larry," I said.

"WHICH LARRY?!?!" he demanded.

"The dead one."

He sighed. "We're getting nowhere here. One of the fish died . . . "

"Yes."

"When you take the dead fish out of the tank, who is that?"

"Who is what?"

"Who is the fish that died?" he asked.

"Larry."

"Which Larry?"

"The dead one."

"Honey, can you tell these fish apart?"

"No."

"So, you don't know which fish died."

"Yes, I do," I said.

"Well, which one is it?"

"The one that was floating at the top of the tank."

"And that fish is . . . "

"Dead."

THE RULE OF THREE

A s a suburban mom, I always expected that in addition to doing laundry, making meals, and butting heads with kids over homework, there would be a fair amount of taxi driving in my job description. What I didn't count on, however, was that my chauffeuring duties would not only include my kids and their friends, but also the assorted pets in my household.

Ignorant me, I had always thought our dog, our lizard, and our chinchilla would just hang out at home in their cages or tanks or sometimes clinging to the living room drapes when they escaped from their cages and tanks. But no, it seemed our animals also had extracurricular activities that necessitated a certain amount of driving (and swearing) on my part.

I realized this one day as I was preparing to go out of town for work for a few days. Riley had an appointment at the doggie salon, and then I planned to board him at the dog walker's house because my husband and the kids wouldn't be home to let him out all day and I didn't have anyone else who could come in and do it. But as the Beckerman bus was pulling out of the driveway, Josh informed me that Einstein was scheduled to do a guest appearance at school that day.

"Can't we reschedule Einstein?" I said. "It took me two weeks to get Riley a grooming appointment and he needs it before he goes off to the boarder's."

"No, Mom," Josh said impatiently. "You know I had to get double special top security clearance for an exotic animal to come to the school today only!"

I imagined the superintendent of schools and my son's principal doing "rock, paper, scissors" to decide if the lizard could get a one-day middle school visa.

"Well, the dog's appointment is at ten, he has to get to the boarder's by three-thirty, and the lizard isn't due at the school until two, so I guess I can do it all," I said. I had a frightening list of things to do before I left town, but I was foolishly confident that I could make it all work without imploding.

Giddy with my multitasking capabilities, I dropped the kids off at school, the dog off at the groomer's, and swung by my house to pick up the dry cleaning and feed Henry the chinchilla. When I gazed into the chinchilla mansion, I noticed that Henry looked a little listless. He could have just been sleepy since he usually slept in the afternoons, but since I didn't want to come home from my trip to a dead chinchilla, I decided to run him over to the vet to get him checked out. The problem was, they didn't have an appointment until 1:00 p.m.

Now here's where things got hairy.

1:00 p.m.: I brought the chinchilla to the vet. They said he was just low-energy. While we were there, I got a call from the groomer's that the dog was ready.

1:45 p.m.: I threw the chinchilla back in the car and ran home to get the lizard.

1:55 p.m.: No time to drop off the chinchilla. I scooped up the lizard in his travel cage and brought him to school. The chinchilla was making a weird noise. I suspected he wanted off the bus.

2:20 p.m.: Back at the groomer's to pick up the dog. I still had the chinchilla in the car, and now also the dog.

2:50 p.m.: No time to drop off the chinchilla and the dog. Went back to school to get the lizard and the kids.

3:10 p.m.: No time to drop off the lizard, the chinchilla, the dog, and the kids. Stopped at the pet shop to get more dog food for the boarder and crickets for the lizard.

I now had two kids, a dog, a lizard, a chinchilla, and sixty crickets in the car. I started praying that I didn't get stopped by a cop for anything because there was no way I could explain this scenario without being subjected to a breathalyzer.

3:30 p.m.: I dropped the dog off at the boarder's, the kids at their after-school activities, and the lizard, the chinchilla, and the crickets back at the house.

Later that night when my husband got home, I was collapsed prone on the couch.

"How was your day, honey?" he asked.

I glared at him. "Ruff."

....

Don't get me wrong . . . I am an ardent dog lover. I cry at dog movies, volunteer at pet adoption days, and spend more money on specialty dog food for our pet than I spend on groceries for my family.

But there have been some dogs in my past who gave the art of being a good dog a bad name.

It started with a Schnauzer next door named Lucky. I was pretty sure Lucky was a member of the doggie mafia. He was sweet and obedient around his family, but if you weren't family, he would get so mean you'd think he might take a hit out on you. Lucky clearly saw my seven-year-old self as some kind of threat to his family because every time I would stop by to ask their kids to come out and play, Lucky would appear snarling and snapping at the door and throw himself into the screen so hard, I was sure he would bust through and eat my face off. It got to the point where I decided that there were plenty of fish in the sea and I didn't need these kids as my friends if there was a chance that Lucky would give me a pair of cement shoes and turn me into fish bait.

Did I mention that Lucky was a Miniature Schnauzer?

Yeah, John Dillinger was short, too.

We had our own dogs in my family who were loving and sweet, which was the reason I was so surprised to encounter a bad egg like Lucky. I decided they must have called him Lucky because you'd be lucky if you escaped a chance meeting with him with all your fingers intact.

My next run-in with a mean dog was Jade, my ex-boyfriend's Dachshund. Jade was his first girlfriend, and she was really not happy to have a rival in the house. I soon discovered that Jade was two-faced. She was all nice to me in front of him, but the minute he left the room, she would jump up into his empty seat on the couch and start snarling and baring her teeth at me. As soon as he returned, she was my friend again.

When I told my boyfriend, he said, "Sweet Jade? She would never do that!"

But Jade and I knew better. She was a Dachshund with a dark side. I called her Darth Jader.

After this, I concluded it was the small dogs that were danger-ous, and given the chance, they could and would relieve you of your nose. I had a great aunt like that who was so diminutive you could lose her in a club chair, but she had a voice like a megaphone and would routinely yell obscenities from her oversized throne if she thought you weren't up to snuff. Eventually I had my own family and assured my husband that there would be no place in our house for a small, man-eating dog. So, we got Riley, who didn't have a mean bone in his body and I never once heard him growl except when he met Henry. The dog was an eighty-five-pound pushover. He was the doggie version of Charlie Brown. In the dog world, you had your alpha dogs and your beta dogs. Riley was a such a weenie, we decided he was a zeta dog.

Riley had a lot of good dog friends in the neighborhood and in his dog walking group. But when a new family moved onto our street, a dog appeared with them who was not friendly and took an instant dislike to Riley. It was a French Bulldog named, appropriately, Biff, like the bully in the movie, *Back to the Future*. Biff would lunge at any other dog who was within spitting distance of him, straining at his leash, while his owner looked on and said nothing. Coincidentally, whenever I walked Riley, Biff always seemed to be out walking at the same time. Riley, being a big weenie dog, was terrified of the bully Bulldog Biff, and it wasn't long before Biff turned my dog into such a scaredy cat that we started calling him Riley McFly.

Finally, one day, I'd had enough of Biff's bullying ways. As we walked out of our driveway, Biff appeared from around the corner and lunged at Riley, pulling on his leash and yapping and baring his teeth while his owner looked on. I was furious that the owner did nothing to intervene. As Riley cowered behind me, I got between him and Biff and suddenly lunged forward at Biff and growled and barked back. Biff stopped yapping, tucked his tail between his legs, and ran back to his owner's side. The owner also tucked his tail between his legs and took off.

Ultimately, like all bullies, Biff was all bark and no bite.

....

"Hi. Your dog Riley is in my backyard," said a friendly voice on my answering machine. I looked around for the familiar black snoring lump on the floor and realized with a start that the lump was nowhere to be found.

I did recall letting the dog out back to do his business.

I did not recall letting the dog back in.

Still, I couldn't fathom how he had disappeared from our property since our backyard is completely fenced in. I went outside calling his name and walked the perimeter of the back fence. That's when I discovered a distinct lack of fence-ness where a section of our fence had once been in the back corner.

I realized that the dog hadn't pole vaulted over the six-foot fence as I had suspected, or dug his way out underneath it like he was in the movie *The Shawshank Redemption*. He had merely walked through the gaping hole to freedom.

Although I was understandably concerned by this discovery, I was relieved to know that he had merely gone on a jaunt a couple of blocks away and not run off to join the dog circus.

I quickly called the friendly voice back and discovered that my dog was cavorting in her backyard with her dog, and p.s., this was not the first time he had been over there. Not only that, but she reported seeing my dog across the street several times at the homes of two other dogs, as well.

I was stunned. Apparently, Riley had been leading a double life for quite some time. While I thought he had been happily chasing squirrels in our fenced-in backyard, he had actually been several blocks away cavorting with a lady Corgi, canoodling with a female Poodle, and being playful with a pretty Pekingese. On each occasion, he had darted off before the owners could see who he was and returned to our backyard before I could notice his absence.

Could it be that my dog Riley, sweet, *neutered* Riley, was actually a doggie Don Juan? I'd never known Riley to deceive me. What was this new personality trait? Or could it be he was smarter than we all thought? For all I knew Riley had been out robbing banks, or worse yet, robbing pet stores. I wondered if there was a warrant out for his arrest and if he was on the FBI's Ten Most Wanted Retrievers list. He wouldn't have been the first dog that deceived me. When I was growing up, our Golden Retriever Honey used to go into the neighbor's yard and steal bones from the neighbor's dog. It was definitely a dog-eat-dog-world, and Golden Retrievers (or at least the ones I knew) were the unlikely, sweet-faced hoodlums of the canine kingdom.

Recalling the way Riley used to steal socks and underwear from under our noses, I was sure he had not only crossed the fence, he'd crossed the line. I'd bet his Milk Bone dog biscuits on it.

I grabbed his leash and jumped into the car to bring him back to his bachelor pad.

This time the terrier's owner had managed to keep him contained in their backyard and when I got to her house, I found Riley and his lady friend romping together joyfully. Little did she know he had an entire harem on the street.

"Well, I can see why he would want to come over here," I said to the dog's owner. "She's very cute."

"Hmm, he may have come over for her the first time, but after that, I think it was to see me."

"What do you mean?"

"Every time he was here, I tried to catch him to see who he belonged to, but he kept running away from me, so I did the only thing I could think of to get him to come to me."

"What's that?" I wondered.

"I gave him treats."

....

It was actually a good thing that I found out about Riley's excursions when I did. Although I live in the suburbs, we are in an area with a nearby mountain — albeit a small one — and occasionally an errant bear wanders down to our suburban neighborhood to check out the local garbage can offerings. I've never actually seen a bear in our town, but I've heard news reports about them, so I assumed they must be true. Of course, I've heard reports about Sasquatch sightings and alien abductions, too, but I'm not that gullible and have actually only seen an alien once and he didn't abduct anybody.

I recalled a time that a neighbor from around the corner called me to ask if my dog was inside because there was a bear walking down the middle of the street.

"Aren't you going to ask if my kids are inside, too?" I said.

She did not.

Anyway, I was not thinking about bears or Bigfoot or aliens when I took Riley for a walk one morning . . . until he suddenly froze. A low, rumbling growl rolled out of his throat as all the fur on the back of his neck stood up. Then he crouched down as though readying himself for an attack. Alarmed by his behavior, I froze too, and looked around for whatever it was that was making him so nervous. I wasn't that fast and was really concerned that Riley and I would both become bear bait. You'd think I would be comforted by the fact that I had a big dog to protect me, but I knew Riley wouldn't be any help. Although he looked threatening, when push came to shove, or rather push came to bear mauling, he'd likely haul dog butt to the next county before staying to defend me against a bear, or even a chipmunk.

When Joel and I went hiking in the Rockies the previous summer, we took bear bells and bear spray with us on the trails. But I was completely defenseless now as I stood there with the dog and I began to wonder if I'd made a mistake getting a super friendly retriever instead of something more intimidating, like a pet rhinoceros.

The dog continued to growl as I looked in all directions for the bear I was sure was about to come roaring out of the trees and shred me to pieces. Then, suddenly, a door to one of the nearby houses flew open and something came shooting out of the house like a bullet. A moment later, the smallest, fluffiest dog I'd ever seen arrived at my feet, yipping at me like a wind-up toy. Riley and I stood gaping in shock as this little wisp of a dog tried to intimidate us with his formidable, um, fluff.

"Don't worry," yelled an older woman in a housedress and slippers as she came bursting out the same door as the fluffy dog. "He won't attack unless I give him the command."

"This is a guard dog?" I asked her incredulously.

"Yes," she assured me. "He's an Attack Pomeranian."

Honestly, I could never have conceived of those two words being used together in the same sentence. I was floored. And if dogs could laugh, I'd swear Riley was cracking up.

"What does he do to protect you?" I wondered. "Yip the intruder to death?"

"He's very fast," she assured me.

"He has to be . . . so no one steps on him," I responded.

She smiled. "Usually his bark is enough to scare people away," she said. "He sounds much bigger than he is."

I thought he sounded exactly as big as he was, but I didn't want to burst her bubble. At this point the Pomeranian had stopped barking and was busy trying to sniff my dog, who was having none of it. Riley shooed the little dog away from him and nudged me to continue our walk.

"Well, we need to go," I said. "You should take your dog inside, though. I heard there are some bears in the area today."

"Oh, that's not a problem," she said. "My other dog will defend us against bears."

"And that dog would be . . . ?" I wondered.

"A toy Poodle. He's even faster than the Pomeranian."

I smiled. "Well as long as you're faster than the poodle, you should be fine."

....

When your kids are young, it's a given that you, the mommy, have to make the school lunches because it is the only way to ensure your child does not end up making themselves cookie sandwiches or ketchup quesadillas to take to school for lunch, or buying lunch and ordering hot dogs with french fries every single day.

The problem with being the school lunch maker, though, is that I am also the breakfast cooker, the bed maker, the laundry lady, and the caretaker who feeds all of our millions of pets. To do all this, I routinely have to wake up an hour before everyone else to get everything done. Since I am not a morning person, this means there is always a 50/50 chance the kids will end up with dog kibble in their lunch box and the dog will get a PB&J sandwich in his bowl.

Fortunately, by the time my kids hit middle school, I thought I could see the light at the end of the school lunch tunnel. Confident that they finally had the maturity to make good food choices, I decided to give them a crash course in lunch making.

"This is the refrigerator," I said to them after gathering them in the kitchen for School Lunch 101. "It is where we keep the actual food, unlike the pantry, which you are very familiar with, where we keep the stuff that pretends to be food, such as the chips and cookies."

"Okay," they said in unison.

"Here you will find all the things you need to make a sandwich, such as bread, deli meat, lettuce, and mustard."

"How does it all actually get onto the bread?" asked my son.

"You must put it on there, young Padawan," I instructed.

"Ohhh. Okay."

I then pointed to the lowest shelf.

"In this drawer we have the fruit," I continued. "This is real fruit, not like that fruit leather stuff you guys like to chew that can actually be used to repair items in lieu of duct tape. Unlike the fruit leather, the real fruit is actually made from fruit."

"Whoa!" they said incredulously.

"I know. Crazy, right? And it comes from trees! Who'd a thought?"

"Finally, we have the pantry," I continued, escorting them to a nearby cupboard. "You already know the pantry, otherwise known as the Junky Cabinet. It is where we keep the food-esque items that have labels with ingredients no one can pronounce, which enables the items to last into the next millennium."

"These items are what we call 'snacks,'" I continued. "A snack size serving is this much," I said, grabbing a handful of chips. "Not this much," I said as I held up the entire fourteen ounce bag.

They nodded with vague understanding.

"Starting tomorrow, you guys will make your own lunches and in each lunch bag you will have a sandwich, a piece of fruit, a small junky snack, and a bottle of water. If you don't make lunch, you will have no lunch unless you buy it with your own money."

As I explained this whole process, Riley followed me around the kitchen, stopping at each food station to see if something was actually going to be taken out and perhaps, with any luck, dropped on the floor. This has worked numerous times before, often ending with success when he would walk into me and cause me to drop said food item into his waiting jaws. With any luck, it was sliced turkey breast and not broccoli rabe.

"A word of warning," I continued. "There are dangerous dog-infested waters in this kitchen and if you slip while holding a food item, I cannot guarantee that you or the food item will escape unscathed. Many a time I have set sail to make lunch here, only to be overcome by dog pirates who stole my lunch booty."

"Those must be the days we got cheese sandwiches," whispered Emily to her brother.

The kids nodded solemnly. The dog gave them an innocent look. Could a sweet face like that steal their school lunches? You bet your sweet bippy he would.

"So, are we clear on the whole lunch thing now?" I asked.

"Yes!"

"Great," I said. "So, what's for lunch tomorrow?"

"I dunno," said my son. "What are you making?"

....

I'm not generally in the habit of driving around with all my pets in the car. As I mentioned earlier, it had only happened once before when every pet had someplace to be, and fortunately, they'd all made their scheduled appointments without incident.

But then one day it happened again, and this time we were not quite as lucky.

We were all in the car, driving around to warm up. Another freak storm had knocked the power out at our house and after three days of no heat, our house was a refrigerator. I sent the kids off to stay with their grandparents, but decided to stay and wait for the power company to come do the repairs so I could care for the animals. After a few days of no power, it was starting to get pretty cold in the house and I realized I needed to get the pets into a warmer locale. It was not as much of an issue for the dog and the chinchilla because they had thick fur coats. But the lizard was cold-blooded and he needed an external heat source to keep warm. Since I was not that big on the idea of snuggling up to him to share my body heat, I thought the next best thing would be heated car seats.

We had been in the house for nearly seven years and had lost power in varying degrees at least one time during each of those years. Our property was surrounded by towering pine trees that swayed precariously whenever a big snow event moved through. Since the pine trees did not lose their leaves, the snow would pile up on the branches and ultimately, the branches would collapse from the weight, taking down the power lines with them. Sometimes it would take a day or two for the power company to come fix the problem since all our power lines were:

a. above ground,

b. nearly inaccessible by the power company, and

c. held together with spit.

When it first happened (not including the time we had to move with the dog into the hotel) we would make a game of it and light candles, play board games, and eat cold SpaghettiOs out of a can. But after a half dozen years, the recurring power loss had grown tiresome and now that I had a thirteen-year-old and an eleven-year-old, playing Yahtzee around the flashlight had lost some of its charm.

Unfortunately, we had only been out about fifteen minutes and Einstein had just started to thaw, when I found the street blocked by a downed power line. I tried going an alternate route and was blocked again. At the third blockade, I pulled up to a police car to ask for directions around the trouble. I waved him over and he leaned in, but then he noticed the three-foot lizard in my passenger seat and jumped back.

"Excuse me, Ma'am, is that a lizard in your passenger seat?" asked the police officer leaning in my car window. This might not be the strangest question anyone has ever asked, but it's certainly up there in the top ten.

"It is. It's a bearded dragon, actually," I clarified.

The dog was in the back seat. Henry was in a cage next to him. And Einstein was riding shotgun.

"And you're driving him around, why?"

"I need to warm him up," I said. I cupped my hand to my mouth and whispered under my breath, "Cold-blooded."

The police officer nodded.

"What about those two?" he asked, gesturing to the dog and the chinchilla in the back seat.

"They're just along for the ride," I explained.

"Okay," he shrugged. "Is there any place you're trying to get to in particular?"

I realized that the lizard was probably not only cold, but hungry. We had run out of Lizard Chow right when the storm hit and I was unable to get out of the house since.

"I need to get to the pet shop to get some crickets," I said.

"Do you want to drive them around, too?" asked the police officer.

"No, that would be silly," I said. "I need to feed them to the lizard."

"Of course," he said.

"So, how can I get around this mess?" I asked him.

He explained a complicated, circuitous route to me that left me totally confused.

"You got that?" he asked.

"No," I said. "But I've got three other passengers. I'm sure one of them can explain it to me."

....

A month after the freak storm, spring arrived and I was never so grateful for a change of seasons. I felt like we'd been stuck inside for years, instead of months, and I was pretty sure the dog felt the same way. It would still be another four weeks at least until we could open the pool so I decided, in the meantime, to take Riley on some long walks to help him/us get back in shape. He would be turning seven that year, which was nearly as shocking to me as the fact that Emily and Josh would be twelve and fourteen. They had all transitioned from youngsters to teenagers together and it seemed to have happened in a blink. Although Riley was now considered middle-aged, there was nothing about him that suggested he was getting older. He still chased the Frisbee and caught it like a pro and swam in the pool with the kids and their friends until the last friend went home. He did, however, seem to have matured emotionally. Aside from his annual trips to see Dr. Benson for his shots, there'd been no incident in two years that necessitated any emergency doggie E.R. visits or ingested yarn interventions, although he could still be caught red-pawed eating a rock now and then.

When we got back to the house after his walk, I sat at my desk to do some work and Riley lay on the floor by my side to get back to gnawing on a new bone I had bought him. About half an hour later, I heard this sound like someone was letting the air out of a tire. It went on for about five seconds and then stopped. I looked around the room to see if there was a gas leak or something . . . and that's when I smelled it. It was like driving down the industrial section of the New Jersey Turnpike. That's when I realized it *was* a gas leak. But it wasn't a gas leak from the pipes. It was a gas leak from the dog. I looked down at him and saw that he was sleeping. He hadn't moved a muscle. He hadn't even twitched. I wondered how something that noxious could escape from his nether regions and not sear off the hair on his tail.

After changing over his food countless times and putting a lock on the garbage, we hadn't had a problem with the dog's gas issues for years. But in that moment, it became clear that something new must have been introduced into his diet that caused him to pass the kind of gas that was a veritable weapon of mass destruction. And then I remembered I ordered the new bone for him online. It was made of yak milk. Yak, of course, is not an animal we would generally run into in my suburban New Jersey neighborhood, so yak milk was not widely available. This was probably because no one wanted to get close enough to a yak to milk it. But the online pet store I ordered from said yak milk bones are easily digestible and great for big chewers, like Riley. It said nothing about the fact that while yak milk bones might be easily digestible, they have a residual effect that results in a fart that could take out a small nation.

Naturally, I would feel bad if Riley was physically distressed by the Yak Yucks, as I decided to call them. But he seemed completely unfazed by his nuclear butt emissions. It occurred to me that a dog that liked to roll in dead things in the yard probably wouldn't care if he made my house smell like a bog. However, I would feel guilty if he wiped out the entire planet with his gas, which was a distinct possibility considering how it was affecting me.

I decided I needed to consult with Dr. Benson before things got worse, and by worse, I mean caused the paint to peel off my walls and the tile to buckle on my floors. She said if he had no other symptoms than gas, it was okay to give the dog some GasX to remedy the gas leak.

Later, when Joel got home, the dog's gas had dissipated, but the house still smelled a little like a men's locker room after the Super Bowl.

"What's that smell?" he said, pinching his nose.

"We had a gas leak," I said.

"Did you call the gas company?" he said.

"Something like that," I replied.

"What did they say?"

"Shut off the main valve," I said. "And don't give the dog any more yak."

....

I was out walking Riley, keeping an eye out for bears and attack Pomeranians, when a car stopped next to the curb near a small house and a woman got out with a bag of groceries in one hand and an armful of fluff in the other.

"That is a really cute dog!" I exclaimed as she put the fluff down on the ground. The fluff suddenly turned into a dog and did a little happy dance.

"What kind is he?" I asked.

"He's a Schnoodle," she replied happily.

I raised my eyebrows. A flurry of jokes came to mind and I had to bite my lip to make sure I didn't blurt them out loud. But even with my best efforts, one escaped.

"Oh really?" I said. "Vould you like some Veiner schnitzel vith your Schnoodle?"

"What?"

"Um, I mean, what kind of dog is a Schnoodle?" I asked, stifling a giggle. Every time the word *Schnoodle* came out of my mouth, I had this incredible urge to put on lederhosen and yodel.

"It's part Schnauzer and part Poodle," she explained.

"Can I pet him?" I asked.

"Sure!"

I reached down and touched the dog. His coat was surprisingly soft.

"He's really soft," I said as I tickled him under his chin. He wagged his stump of a tail vigorously.

"I know," she agreed. "I love to sit and stroke him."

"You like to sit and stroke your Schnoodle?" I repeated, and then I schnorted. She looked questioningly at me. This was bad. The Schnoodle lady was going to schnock me in the schnose if I kept this up. I needed to change gears.

"Um, what's his name?" I asked her.

"Schneider."

"Schneider? Your Schnoodle's name is Schneider?" I said. Then I burst out laughing.

"What's so funny?"

"Um. I'm sorry. I, uh . . . I had an uncle named Schneider," I lied. "He liked to drink Schnapps."

She narrowed her eyes. Clearly, I was on shaky ground.

"It's just a funny coincidence," I said, giggling again.

This was not the first time I had encountered one of these poodle mixes. I have met Labradoodles, Goldendoodles, Maltipoos, Yorkipoos, Cockapoos, Scoodles, Poogles, and Puggles. Some of these dogs had silly names and some of these dogs were silly looking, but I'd never had a reaction to the names the way I did to the Schnoodle. I knew if I didn't cut it out, the lady was going to sic her Schnoodle on me. Unfortunately, just thinking about this made me laugh again.

I realized I left her kind of hanging and I needed to say something to get out of this conversation. But I was sure that if I said *Schnoodle* again, I was going to schnicker aloud, so I decided to change the subject.

"Do you have any other dogs?" I asked.

"Yes," she said brightly. "We have two others."

"Oh! What are they?"

"They're Schnockers."

"*Schnockers?*"

"Yes," she explained. "They are part Schnauzer and part Cocker Spaniel."

"You have a Schnoodle and two Schnockers?" I asked her, barely containing myself.

"Yeah . . ." she said.

I smiled. "Your husband is a very lucky man!"

BARK TO THE FUTURE

R iley is a big dog. A very big, very black, very hairy dog. Much as we love him to pieces, the big hairy black dog has one down side. He sheds like a yeti. Of course, this isn't a problem if you have someone you dislike you can invite over who's allergic to dog hair, or you're someone who likes to knit with dog fur. However, since I don't fall into any of those categories, the abundance of dog hair is not something that makes me particularly happy.

In general, Riley sheds a lot. But in the spring, he "blows his coat." This is a real thing for double-coated dogs like retrievers who shed their undercoat in what would appear to be a Category five hurricane of dog hair. With one shake of his body, Riley blows so much coat that it feels like we are living in a sci-fi movie called *The Dog Hair That Took Over the Universe*. He sheds so much fur that I'm convinced if we shave him, he would actually turn out to be a Chihuahua. I wouldn't say that I'm completely obsessive about keeping our house clean, but something about all the dog hair transforms me from a quiet, unassuming suburbanite into the Evil Queen of Vacuumville. In the morning, I run the vacuum after breakfast. By lunchtime, the dog hair dust bunnies threaten to take over the house and I have to drag out the vacuum again. Finally, there is one more vacuum run before bed in the hopes that when I wake up the next day the house will still be dog-hair-free. This, of course, never ever happens, and makes me suspect that the dog has an evil plot to shake his fur all over my house while I sleep just so he can see me freak out in the morning. The irony is that the dog is deathly afraid of the vacuum cleaner. I don't recall him having had any traumatic encounters with the vacuum when he was a puppy, so I'm not sure what it is about the vacuum that scares him, except maybe the really loud noise and the fact that it sucks up everything that it comes in contact with, which, on the very rare occasion, sometimes includes his tail. As an aside, he is also afraid of the bags the dry cleaning comes in, umbrellas, and helium balloons, so I suppose in the grand scheme of things, a vacuum cleaner is his most mundane phobia.

I was trying to figure out if there was another way to keep the house dog-hair-free short of installing wall-to-wall carpeting that matched all the dog hair. Then, as I was watching TV and running the vacuum, the vacuum gods bestowed a gift on me. There, on my screen, was a commercial for a new gadget called a robot vacuum. It was a fabulous new invention that looked like a giant hockey puck and would run around the house on one charge, collecting dog hair and furry dust bunnies from every corner, with nary a push or a shove from me. In the same way that Superman could sense villains, the robot vacuum could sense dog hair and dust and would immediately set out on a mission to seek, suck up, and destroy.

I went online and immediately ordered the vacuum, express delivery. The next day my robotic vacuum arrived. I plugged it in and let it go. It was awesome. It sucked up all the dog hair faster than the dog could shed it and my house was a shiny thing of shedless beauty. But just when I was ready to celebrate, I realized we had a bigger problem. While Riley was not a fan of the regular vacuum, the new robotic one completely stressed him out. And when he got stressed, he shed. And since the vacuum was running all day, the dog shed much more . . . which made the robotic vacuum cleaner run more . . . which made the dog shed more. In my effort to solve a problem, I had created a larger one. You've heard of the Circle of Life? This was the Circle of Fur.

At dinner that night, I told Joel my dog hair tale of woe.

"I can't keep up with all the dog hair," I said to him. "And the robot vacuum seems to be making things worse."

"So, what are you going to do?" he replied. "Get rid of the dog?"

"Of course not," I said. "But there has to be something else I can do."

"You've been going about this all wrong, Mom," said Josh through a mouthful of barbecue spareribs. Riley sat at Josh's feet waiting for some morsel of sparerib to find its way down to the floor.

"What do you mean?" I asked.

"You need to take out the middleman," he said with the absolute authority of a fourteen-year-old.

"What does that mean?" I said.

"You've been vacuuming the floor."

"Yeah?" I said.

He wiped his mouth. "Instead you should go to the source and just vacuum the dog."

....

Vacuuming isn't the only chore I dread. I'm pretty much an equal opportunity chore hater. This is in direct conflict with my need to have everything neat, clean, and organized. Then there are my kids who prefer to keep everything messy, dirty, and disorganized, so I have to sacrifice my dislike of chores to keep my house put together. It occurred to me, if I made the kids do the chores, not only would I get out of doing them myself, but the house would also be less messy because they wouldn't want to have to clean up after themselves. It seemed like a win-win until I realized I still couldn't even get them to make their beds, so the likelihood that I could get them to do laundry and clean the bathroom was about as great as the chance I could get the dog to pooper-scoop the backyard.

The dinner cleanup is the only help I actually got from everyone, which is probably because they know they wouldn't get fed otherwise. Joel set down the rules early on that everyone who eats the food has to help with the cleanup, so it's a pretty speedy affair. It also doesn't hurt that we have three dishwashers. First there is the electronic one which does a pretty good job, assuming you pre-wash the dishes before you run them through the dishwasher. Then there's dishwasher number two — Joel. He's generally responsible for the hand wash, the pots, pans, and cooking utensils that don't go in the dishwasher. Having spent a summer at sleepaway camp when he was sixteen and worked as, you guessed it, a dishwasher, he considers himself an expert in the field. At the end of a meal, he will throw himself into his work with such gusto that it almost seems like he's participating in an Olympic event. The kids are on drying duty for the hand wash, and typically do a good job when they aren't whipping each other in the butts with wet dish towels.

The third dishwasher in the house is the dog. Of all three, Riley ranks best for getting the dishes completely free of food, although I wouldn't want to eat off the dishes he cleans. The problem, though, is not so much the dishes he licks when they're dirty. It's the dishes he licks when they're clean. For some reason, in addition to a penchant for chicken, carrots, and socks, Riley also has developed a taste for dishware. I thought that since he knew the dishes were dirty going in, maybe he theorized that they would also be dirty coming out. Who knows. I don't speak dog or I'd ask him.

Whatever his motivation, the upshot was that whenever I attempt to empty the dishwasher, I have to body-block the dog to get to the dishes before he does. Unfortunately, the dog is at dishwasher level, and I am not, so he has the upper hand, er, paw, in the race to the dishes.

"Beat it Riley," I barked at him one morning as I lowered the dishwasher door. He ignored me. He had been trained to "sit," "stay," and "fetch me a Diet Coke," but "beat it" was not part of his repertoire. He moved a little closer to the dishwasher and I tried to put myself between the dog and the dishes. It occurred to me that most dog owners have to worry about their dogs chasing cars, not licking the clean dishes, and I marveled at how *unique* our dog was, and by unique I mean *weird*.

"Riley, move," I said more aggressively. This time he listened . . . and moved to the other side of the dishwasher where he had better access. Technically, he did what I'd said, so I couldn't be mad. I quickly stepped over the dishwasher door and stood in front of him, and then picked up one of the dinner dishes to move it out of his reach.

"Listen buddy," I said, waving a dish at him. "These dishes are clean. There is no food on them. They are an empty promise of a snack that has long since been washed away by time and Cascade. This is not a dish. It's a dream. Time to let go."

The dog admitted defeat and finally moved away from the machine. I stepped around him to get back into a better unloading position, failing to notice that I had created a small puddle on the floor from the not-quite-dry dishes. Naturally, I slipped on the puddle, bobbled the plate, and dropped the clean dish onto the floor where it broke into a million pieces.

I shrugged.

One less dish for the dog to lick.

....

As spring segued into summer and the dog's extreme shedding sub-sided, I thought I had finally overcome our furry dust issues. But then one night I saw a dust bunny out of the corner of my eye as it darted from under the entertainment unit in the family room around the corner and into the kitchen. I was pretty sure it was a dust bunny. However, even I realized it's pretty unusual to see a dust bunny with a clear agenda, and this one seemed like it definitely had a destination in mind. Still, I decided to give the dust bunny the benefit of the doubt.

"Did you see that?" I asked Emily, who was sitting on the couch next to me.

"See what?" she replied.

"A thing," I said, pointing in the direction of the kitchen.

"What thing?" she said. I turned and saw the dust bunny emerge from the kitchen, look at me, and then nonchalantly walk down the steps into the breakfast room.

"That thing," I said, pointing to the sashaying dust bunny.

She screamed and stood up on the couch, which seemed redun-dant since we were already on the couch. But it seemed like the appropriate response, nonetheless, so I did it, too.

"What is it?" she asked. We both watched the dust bunny saunter over to Riley's bed and hop on. The actual owner of the bed was asleep at our feet and seemed unbothered that an aggressive dust bunny had taken over his domain.

"It's a dust bunny," I said.

"No, it's not," she said. "It's a mouse."

"Actually, it's not a mouse. It has no tail. I think it's a vole."

"When did you become an expert on rodents?" she said.

"When they started coming in from outside pretending to be dust bunnies," I replied.

It was true. This wasn't the first time we'd had a vole in the house. However, it was the first time we'd had one that was brazen enough to strut around like he owned the place. In the past when we discovered a vole in the house, Joel and I had a division of duties. I would scream and get hysterical, and he would set the live traps. This time however, it was just me and Emily so there was twice the screaming and zero trapping.

"What should we do?" Emily asked.

"I think we should wake up the dog," I replied.

"But he'll hurt the vole," she protested.

"No, if we open the door, he'll just chase it out of the house."

"Okay," she agreed.

I jumped off the couch and went to the back door off the family room and propped it open. A blast of hot air rushed in. I wondered if anyone had ever died of heat stroke while trying to chase a vole out of the house and realized that best case scenario, we get rid of the vole; worst case, we die but we get into Ripley's Believe it or Not.

"All right, wake the dog!" I said.

Riley was a world-class squirrel chaser, so we had high hopes that this would end quickly.

"Riley," Emily yelled, nudging the dog awake. "Look!" She pushed the dog toward his bed. He stood there quizzically, not seeing the intruder. Then, suddenly, the vole moved. The fur on the back of the dog's neck stood up. The vole, on high alert, took two tentative steps across the dog bed. Riley, in response, took one step back, tucked his tail between his legs, and ran out the open back door.

Emily and I stood dumbfounded.

"Now what?" she asked.

"Now . . ." I replied. "We have a new pet."

....

The problem with Henry the chinchilla was that while Emily wanted to snuggle and cuddle with Henry, Henry did not want to snuggle and cuddle with Emily, or really anyone else for that matter. We'd read that chinchillas were very friendly, but it seemed Henry was the odd chinchilla out and was pretty much anti-people from the get-go. He would tolerate Emily for a short time, but eventually he'd start to wriggle and then bite her. As you can imagine, this did not sit particularly well with Emily, or with me for that matter, because not too long after this started to happen, Emily declared that Henry was now the "family" pet and I was somehow appointed his new caretaker, as though I wasn't already doing all the chinchilla maintenance before.

There have been a lot of things written about how kids beg for pets and then it's the mom who ends up taking care of them. Apparently, I missed those articles because I was convinced that my kids would be responsible for all the animals. Before long, however, I was cleaning up after the lizard, cleaning up after the chinchilla, and cleaning up after the dog. Fortunately, Joel cleaned up after himself (for the most part), or I would have resigned my post.

Of all the pets who made messes, though, Henry was the worst. Like any rodent, he seemed to do his business all the time. A little pellet would come out with every step he took until his crate was filled with an entire floor-full of poop pellets and cedar shavings. This would have been bad enough, but Henry was also a chucker. He would stand in the crate and use his back feet to chuck everything on the floor of the crate out onto the floor of the breakfast room. Maybe he was unhappy with the accommodations or the housekeeping, or maybe he just wanted to share the wealth. Who knows, but as the Chinchilla-Chucker-Cleaner-Upper, I was not pleased.

So, now we had a pet that bit everyone, pooped all day, and then chucked it on the floor. Call me crazy, but at this point I was thinking it was time for Henry to go find another family to torment.

Someplace where he could be free to be himself, but not on my family room floor.

And then along came Dylan.

Dylan was Emily's friend who really loved Henry, and oddly enough, Henry, the equal opportunity biting chinchilla, did not bite Dylan. And thus, I had a plan. I checked it over with Joel and then took the plunge.

"Hey Em, can I talk to you about something?" I asked her as I stood in the doorway to her room.

Although she had just segued into teenagerhood, she still had an abundance of stuffed animals strewn across her comforter that fought her for bed rights when it came time for her to go to sleep. She had a fluffy pink rug, stained in places by magic markers that said they were non-staining. And her walls and doorways were decorated with whimsical fairy appliqués that had been there since I put them up when we bought the house. Before we moved out of our first house when Emily was three, she'd had similar fairies on her walls in her bedroom there. When we told her we'd be moving she was distraught.

"What about my fairies?" she'd asked tearfully. "What's gonna happen to them?" The fairies had always been part of her nighttime ritual. Before bed, Joel would pick Emily up and fly her around the room so she could kiss each fairy goodnight.

"When we say goodbye to this house, the fairies are going to fly to our new house and go on your walls in your new bedroom," Joel had told her.

Three months later, Joel and Emily stood in her empty bedroom and she said goodbye to the only home she'd ever known. In the meantime, I worked furiously in the new house applying a new set of identical fairies to her bedroom walls. When they got back home, Emily ran up to her new bedroom and cried out, "They're here! My fairies are here! I knew they would come!"

It was, truly, the best parenting moment ever.

Now I stood in her doorway and asked the fairies to help me convince Emily to part ways with Henry, but they stayed stubbornly silent. I had given them a new life in this house, but apparently, they were fair-weather fairies.

"What's up?" she asked without looking up from her homework.

"I wanted to talk to you about Henry."

"What about him?"

I sat down on the bed next to her. "It seems like Henry doesn't get a lot of attention these days and I'm wondering if our house is the best place for him."

She put down her pencil and looked at me. "He doesn't get a lot of attention because he bites."

"I know. I'm sorry he didn't turn out to be the kind of pet you'd hoped for, pussycat, but it seems like there *is* one person that Henry really likes."

"Who?"

"Your friend Dylan."

"Oh yeah," she replied. "Henry really likes Dylan. And Dylan really likes Henry, too."

"Do you think Dylan would maybe want Henry to be his pet?"

"Yeah, probably."

"And how would you feel about that?"

"That would be okay," she said. "I would just be glad Henry would be going to a good home." She went back to doing her homework, signaling to me that as far as she was concerned the decision was made and the conversation was over.

I don't know what exactly I had expected. Sadness? Tears? Resistance? But Emily had moved on emotionally from Henry when he'd been relocated to the breakfast room and this, for her, was an end to a relationship that had never really worked for her in the first place.

I, however, was a little bit weepy. I sucked at closure . . . even if the relationship was with a bed-chucking, finger-biting chinchilla. I thought that if I were more self-aware, I'd probably realize that this was the first big change in our family of seven since we got the pets, and it may have unknowingly touched a nerve about all the other changes that would inevitably come down the road for me as everyone got older.

I quickly got over it though and the next time Dylan was over and holding Henry, I made the move.

"Hey Dylan, unfortunately we're going to have to give up Henry and we're looking for a new home for him. Would you be interested in becoming his new owner?"

Dylan looked like his ship had just come in. Henry also seemed to perk up at this news. Either that, or he sensed Emily was near and he was getting his chompers ready for action.

"I would *love* to have Henry," he said. "I just need to check with my mom."

I gave him a rundown of the care and feeding of a pet chinchilla and he didn't seem to mind at all that Henry routinely chucked his bedding on the floor. I'm sure that was because he knew his mother would clean it up.

Half an hour later we had a deal. When Dylan's mom showed up to take Dylan and Henry home, I called out to Emily.

"Hey Em, Henry is leaving for his new digs. Do you want to say goodbye?"

She turned to Henry and said a cursory goodbye. Then she turned to me.

"So, now can we get a cat?"

....

With Henry gone, all the fish dead, and Einstein spending his days in quiet seclusion, happily sunning himself on a heat rock in his tank, Riley again became the center of the pet universe in our house. This meant I could go back to buying multitudes of dog toys without feeling like I was cheating on the other pets. Although it occurred to me that maybe I did it out of guilt for those times I had to leave him home alone while I ran out to go shopping, do errands, or whatever, it didn't stop me from overindulging him. So what if I bribe my dog with squeaky, fuzzy, and tuggy things? I do the same thing with my kids and they seem okay with it.

The only downside to all these purchases is that while I have been somewhat successful in getting my kids to put their stuff away, I have had no such luck with my dog. I actually can't get Joel to put his toys away either, but that's another story. I wasn't sure what the issue was, but much as I tried, Riley could not seem to pick up the command "put away." I had seen videos of other retrievers racing around their houses, picking up their toys, and dumping them in a toy bin, before going to the kitchen, opening the fridge, and getting their owner a beer. The only thing I'd ever seen Riley pick up was dirty socks, and the one time he'd somehow gotten the refrigerator door open, he stood up on his hind legs and ate the remainder of a roast chicken I'd made the night before, half a leftover peanut butter and jelly sandwich, and a pack of individually wrapped cheddar cheese slices. In his defense, he did bring me one of the cheese slices, but I think it was just to help him get the plastic wrapper off. Then, naturally, he threw it all up on the rug.

The main thing I learned from this experience, besides making sure that the refrigerator door was always firmly shut, was to expect less in the way of help around the house . . . and to only get Riley nonedible toys.

Fortunately, now that he was what the vet described as middle-aged, she told me he was much less likely to do anything he wasn't supposed to, like jump on the furniture or get into the garbage or snack off the kitchen counter.

I actually did think he had turned a corner. Then one day we were in our usual rush to get to school and Emily only had time for about three bites of her bagel. I left the rest on the plate so I could wrap it up and put it away for her for later. Then I pushed it to the back of the counter so as not to tempt a hungry, four-legged member of our household who was usually very well-behaved, but could be tempted by the little-known mischievous Bagel Elf. Satisfied that the counter was sufficiently dog-proofed, I whisked her off to school. Ten minutes later I got home and went into the kitchen to wrap up the rest of the bagel.

But when I looked at the plate, there was no bagel.

I have been known to do things and forget that I did them, especially since I was on the cusp of perimenopause and often found myself walking into a room and then immediately forgetting what I had walked in for. So, I checked the garbage to make sure I hadn't actually thrown the bagel out.

No bagel.

Then I looked in the fridge to see if I had wrapped the bagel up and put it in there.

No bagel.

I was utterly at a loss for what could have happened to the bagel. I briefly wondered if the dog had eaten it, but I quickly tossed out that idea. The plate was still all the way at the back of the counter. The counter was a good three feet off the floor. The dog was not all that big. And he has never, ever snacked off the counter. But just to be sure, I called him over so I could assess the situation. He trotted over. He sat down. He looked up at me quite innocently.

And that is when I saw it.

Our good dog . . . the one who has not done anything he is not supposed to . . . that dog had cream cheese smeared all over his face.

I was stunned. Shocked. Dismayed.

"Riley, did you eat the bagel?" I asked, wagging my finger at him. He stuck out his tongue and in one clean sweep, licked the remaining cream cheese off his muzzle.

"Yeah, too little too late," I said to him. "You're already busted."

Shaking my head in disbelief, I went off to clean up the house. As I passed the living room, I peered in and noticed that some of the pillows on the couch were askew, so I went in to straighten them out.

And that is when I saw it: cream cheese smeared all over the velvet pillows on the good couch.

You don't have to be Sherlock Holmes to figure out what went down while I was out of the house. The dog stole the bagel off the counter, took it into the living room, and ate the contraband bagel on the forbidden couch.

I picked up the phone to call Joel to tell him what happened, and while I was still talking to him, I went back into the family room to confront the dog. But in my haste to reprimand the scofflaw, I forgot all about the dog-toy minefield. Although I generally am used to looking down when I walk around this area so as not to trip over or step on the dog, his toys, or the occasional puddle of doggie puke, this time I was not as observant and failed to notice one of the larger dog accessories right in my path. How I could miss a rubber bone that was almost as big as my leg, I'm not quite sure. But before you could say "down boy," I was sprawled on the floor with a fat lip the size of Texas.

I know there are some women who pay a lot of money for lip fillers to plump up their pouts. But I have been naturally blessed with big lips so this was not really a feature I needed to enhance.

Peeling myself off the floor, I ran into the bathroom to look in the mirror. There was no disguising it. I had Trout Mouth.

"Is everything okay?" Joel asked when I got back on the phone. "I heard a yell, a curse, and a thunk."

I tried to say, "I fell on the dog's bone and I got a fat lip," but that's not what came out.

"I thell on the dog'th mone and I got a that lit," I said.

"What?"

"I thell and I got a thatt lit," I repeated, thinking if I yelled he would understand.

"You *thell?*" he said. "What's a *thell?* Honey, you're not making any sense."

I decided to try a different tack. "I tritt on a mone!"

"You *tritt?* Huh?"

I thought that maybe I should just simplify to get my point across. "I hurt my lit."

"What is a *lit?*" he demanded.

I sighed. This was almost more painful than the lip itself. I was at a loss. Was there any way to communicate to my husband what happened that did not require the use of an F, an S, or a P?

"I got hurt," I told him.

"Oh. Are you okay?"

"Yeah. But I got a *that lit.*"

He sighed. "I'm sorry honey, I just can't understand you."

I threw up my arms in defeat and then thrust the phone at the guilty party.

"Here. Talk to the dog."

....

As Riley got older, he seemed to develop more fears. I could relate. As a kid, I used to love rollercoasters, but as an adult I didn't even like to go down the slide at the playground anymore. In my defense, it was probably because the slide was metal and one run down the slide in shorts could leave you with third-degree burns on your butt. I always wondered what numbskull playground designer had thought that would be a good idea. Clearly it was someone who didn't have children, or skin on the back of their legs.

One of the things Riley was not a big fan of, besides vacuums and helium balloons, was elevators. He spent most of his time in a house, so elevators were not typically part of his day-to-day existence.

Fortunately, Riley was fairly adaptable, and after I gave him a load of treats every time we took an elevator, he realized pretty quickly that riding an elevator was not only a tasty endeavor, it was also a great social event. He knew he could count on lots of people giving him lots of attention, which, for a dog, is a pretty cool thing. This being the case, most of our elevator excursions were uneventful. But then one day we got on an elevator during elevator rush hour and it stopped on nearly every floor. I tried to get the dog as close to me as possible to allow for other passengers, but by the time we got down to the tenth floor from twenty, the elevator was almost completely filled up.

Finally, one more person jammed in and we knew that was the last person we could possibly get on before we declared the elevator a clown car.

The last man who jammed himself in stood directly in front of us. His fine tan leather briefcase hung off his shoulder, inches from Riley's face. It looked new and I could smell the leather from where I stood. Apparently, so could Riley, and world class sniffer that he is, he leaned forward to get a good whiff of the briefcase.

Then he licked it.

I was aghast. Fortunately, Riley was a quiet licker and briefcase man didn't seem to notice what had happened. I pulled Riley back and whispered, "No." But apparently, the call of the leather was too much for him, and before I could stop him, he leaned forward and licked the briefcase again. This time it wasn't a short lick. It was one long swipe with his tongue across the entire bottom of the briefcase.

I pulled the dog back again and noticed a wide swath of dog drool, the exact width and length of my dog's tongue, discoloring the base of the briefcase. There was really no hiding it, and I knew it was just a matter of time before the owner of the briefcase discovered the evidence.

I panicked, trying to come up with a solution before we got to the ground floor.

But just before we got to the bottom, one more person pushed into the elevator, juggling a cup of coffee in one hand and a grocery bag in the other. As she stepped across the threshold, she tripped and lurched forward, spilling her coffee across briefcase-man's jacket, his shoes, and his fine leather, dog-drool-stained briefcase.

I looked down at the dog and smiled.

"You are one lucky dog," I whispered to him.

He looked at me and wagged his tail. Then he licked the coffee off the guy's shoes.

....

Before my brother Rich and his wife Paula had kids, they decided their first baby would be a dog. Like me, there was no question in my brother's mind that he would get a Golden Retriever, and within two weeks of making up their minds, they brought home Clyde. Clyde was about as goofy as they come and one of the sweetest dogs I'd ever known. Right from the beginning, he was my brother's dog, and anywhere Rich went in the house, Clyde was only a few steps behind, or more typically, under foot. But Clyde's absolute favorite place to be was out back, under the towering apple tree, sort of like Ferdinand the bull who would spend his time smelling flowers under a big cork tree. When my nephew Jordan was born, he, like most toddlers, had a limited vocabulary. But if you asked him where Clyde was, he would tell you with absolute certainty, "Clyde outside."

Clyde had been around for several years before Riley joined our family, so we thought being around him would give us a good idea of what we could expect from dog ownership. We had two crab apple trees in our own backyard, and I was convinced that eating apples was a retriever thing and we'd have to closely monitor Riley to make sure he didn't overindulge. As it turned out, though, eating apples was a Clyde thing. Riley had more of an appetite for grubs.

Still, the two dogs became good buddies and it was nice that when the cousins would get together to play, the dogs did too. When Rich and Paula came to visit, they always brought Clyde. When we went to see them, we always brought Riley. When we all went to Vermont to ski together, we brought both dogs. There was never any discussion of not including them. The only issue, as far as I was concerned, was the fact that two retrievers made for twice the dog hair and after a visit, I would have to get the leaf blower out to blast all the dog hair out the back door.

When Clyde was about eleven, arthritis suddenly began to creep into his hips and his face rapidly started to turn white.

"Poor Clyde is turning into an old man," said Rich when his family came over for dinner one night. Clyde was under the glass dining room table with Riley, vying for floor rights to any dropped food that entered their domain.

"Yeah, but he still has a lot of pep in his step," I said to him.

"He's definitely slowing down though," he said. "He doesn't really run much anymore."

"Neither do I," I said. "It happens to all of us."

He smiled. "Maybe it happens to you, but it's not happening to me," he said. "I'm staying young, Clyde is staying young, and the kids are staying young."

"Yeah, you keep telling yourself that," I replied.

Less than a year later, Rich called to tell me that Clyde had passed. He was the first pet my brother ever had on his own, and Rich was so attached to him that when Clyde died, I thought the hole left behind in my brother's heart would never heal. But eventually, like anyone who has ever loved and lost a dog, Rich and Paula were able to remember Clyde with joy instead of sorrow, and the stories of the dog's antics became family lore.

A year after they lost Clyde, I wasn't surprised when a new Golden Retriever puppy was welcomed into my brother's family. Right from the beginning, Elvis was his own dog, with a very different personality than Clyde, who would sit in my brother's leather armchair like a person, as though waiting for someone to bring him a cigar and a beer. Elvis liked blueberries and ice cream, would tackle anyone who walked in the door with huge dog hugs, and, like his predecessor, adored my brother best of all. Rich knew there could never be another Clyde. But just like you make room in your heart for another child, Rich had more than enough love in him to let another dog fill the void left by Clyde.

When Clyde passed, it took them all some time to mourn before they could say their goodbyes. But then one day, my brother, his wife, and their two kids spread Clyde's ashes under the old apple tree in the backyard, and damn if that tree didn't stand a little taller after that.

THE LIFE OF RILEY

Although he was clearly getting older, Riley still seemed very much a puppy and would chase a rubber ball or a Frisbee for as long as someone kept throwing it to him or until he dropped dead of exhaustion, whichever came first. I had friends with similarly aged dogs who said they noticed their dogs had begun to slow down, but Riley didn't seem to know how old he was or care. Having a dog that seemed frozen in time made it easier for me to pretend that everything in my life was frozen in time, even though when we first got Riley both kids were in elementary school and now Josh was in his sophomore year of high school and Emily was finishing up middle school. Every once in a while, it struck me that Josh would be in college in three years, and I found it unfathomable that he had been just seven when we got the dog and now he was driving, dating, and sporting something that looked suspiciously like facial hair.

Emily, in turn, was in what I fondly referred to as The Drama

Years when everything that happened in middle school was either a major social crisis or a cataclysmic boy-related event. When she went off to summer camp months before, she'd had pigtails and braces and still supported the stick figure of a little girl. When she got off the bus four weeks later, her hair was artfully blown dry, she had makeup on, and she had sprouted both breasts and hips. Joel and I didn't even realize it was her when she got off the bus behind Josh, and we had to do a double take when she waved at us and yelled hi. Joel took one look at Emily, and then turned to me and quietly mouthed the words, "Oh. My. God."

With that, we knew everything had changed, whether we wanted it to or not.

In this new stage of their lives, it was hard for me not to notice that the kids needed me less than they had before. Instead of confiding in me, they confided in their friends, and even sometimes in each other. I often found out about boyfriend and girlfriend news second- or thirdhand, when one of their friends would let something fly in my company that would result in a dirty look from one of my kids, followed by a reluctant explanation. When I complained to my wise older parents, they reminded me that I had been the same way, and I could expect that, for a while, my kids would move away from me, but then, eventually, they would come back into the fold. I asked if that would happen before or after I moved into an assisted living facility and forgot who they all were.

With all that was going on in their lives, Josh and Emily were definitely spending less time with the dog, except when summer rolled around and they would all return to the pool with their friends, and Riley would join along as though he, too, was in middle school and had as much right to be there as they did.

I had no doubt that the dog thought of himself as one of the kids. In the winter when we took trips skiing, I would bring him to the mountain to drop them off and then go clomping through the snow with him on the designated trails. In the fall, we would go hiking in the nearby nature preserve and Riley would race ahead of the kids, barking at them to keep up as we hit an uneven incline that caused us to trip over protruding roots of old trees that he had easily navigated. Even if Joel and I noticed time passing by ever more quickly, the dog did not, and we both fully expected that he would be one of those large dogs who beat the odds and lived well into his teenage years.

With the kids spending less and less time in the house, Joel and I often found ourselves with more time alone. It was just us and the dog, and I had a strong premonition of what our lives would look like in the not so distant future. For the most part, we got along pretty well and started to rediscover the things we loved about each other without the distraction of the kids and their needs all the time. But then there was the other part, when we were totally sick of each other and were just looking for a fight.

And then it happened. After nearly twenty years of marriage, Joel and I got into a big argument. And it was about, of all things, dirty dog balls.

"I saw you throwing the ball for the dog outside this morning," I said to him one Saturday morning while the kids were sleeping. It was nine o'clock in the morning, which meant they probably wouldn't emerge from their zombie state until sometime around one o'clock. Joel was standing in the kitchen making himself some eggs while Riley lay panting on the floor.

"I did!" he said enthusiastically.

"You used the wrong ball," I said, walking past him to pet the panting dog.

"What do you mean?"

"You threw the green ball that has the treats inside," I said. "You're supposed to throw the yellow ball with no treats."

"What are you, the Fetch Police?" he said, as he flipped his omelet.

"No, but when you use the green ball, the treats inside get dirt and dog drool all over them."

He shook his head at me. "I don't understand. Don't the treats get dog drool all over them when the dog eats them?"

"Yes. But this is dirty dog drool."

"Is there such a thing as clean dog drool?"

"I'm serious," I said.

"I'm not going to stop using the green ball," he said. "It has a better bounce than the yellow ball and he likes to catch it on the bounce."

I glared at him.

"But then you have to wash it and it ruins the treats inside," I said and stormed out of the room. Then I stopped, turned, and yelled over my shoulder. "And they're organic!"

I shouldn't belittle the importance of this topic. The dog's favorite toy is the green rubber ball with the treats inside. When he pushes it across the floor with his nose, the treats will come out of a hole on each end. According to the dog toy people, this is supposed to be very intellectually stimulating for dogs, which would mean at least one member of the family was being intellectually stimulated while another two-thirds of us were spending our time fighting over dog balls.

The problem was, when my husband threw the green ball outside, it would get filthy and the treats inside would also get filthy. Then he'd wash the ball, which made the treats inside wet, and when that happened, they wouldn't come out when the dog pushed his ball across the floor. Then I'd have to fish out the yucky wet treats from a little hole in the ball with my pinky finger and be really annoyed because, undoubtedly, this was the most pressing issue on the planet at the moment.

The dog seemed completely unbothered by all this fuss. Yellow ball . . . green ball . . . he didn't care. As long as someone threw the balls for him, he was happy. For my husband and me though, this was becoming an issue of the utmost importance. It was clear our marriage was going to the dogs.

I stewed in the other room for a while but then realized that we promised to stick together in sickness and in health, and through yellow balls and green balls — although I didn't recall that one being in our marriage vows. Still, I thought it would be best if we tried to be adults and worked out our ball issues.

"Hey honey, I'm sorry I barked at you about the dog balls," I said as I came back into the room. "It's stupid. And really, I'm just thankful that through all these years we still have each other."

"And I'm thankful for you, too," he said and kissed me. "The dog has a lot to be thankful for, too," said my husband.

"What?" I said.

He smiled. "At least he has two balls."

....

When Josh was wrapping up his junior year of high school, things began to get very busy around our house. We met with a college advisor to help him prepare for his SAT tests and to begin narrowing down the list of colleges he would apply to. I was flabbergasted that we were at this stage in his life. The last ten years had flown by like a blur. I remembered that when the kids were younger, I felt like time would last forever. Life had been a series of pool parties and sleepover dates, summer camps and family vacations, braces, glasses, and then contact lenses. It was the same movie played on a loop over and over with little variation, until suddenly it wasn't. I blinked and now Josh was looking at schools that were a plane ride away, and I realized that his life was soon to be his own.

Although we were still over a year away from his departure, he'd already begun the process of going through his things to decide what would eventually go with him and what would stay behind.

But as I helped him figure out which of his belongings were college worthy, I realized there was a big elephant in the room to deal with upon his departure.

Or to be more precise, a big lizard.

Although Einstein was obviously a genius, we did not expect that he would get into the same college as Josh, or any college for that matter, so it was clear he was not going to be tagging along for any dorm parties or fraternal hazing. It was also unlikely that the schools would let him in because that would open the door to pet potbelly pigs and comfort cows, among other unique animal friends. That left it up to me to become Einstein's caretaker and personal manager. In the past few years, I'd passed the cricket baton to Josh, who could now drive, and he'd become one hundred percent responsible for the care and feeding of (and cleaning up after) his bearded dragon. This was just fine with me as I'd never had an emotional attachment to Einstein. He was, after all, a cold-blooded animal so, by his very nature, he was not inclined to be warm and fuzzy. But Josh and Einstein had been together for many years and had a bond of sorts that comes with sharing a room together and being there for each other. Einstein sat on Josh's shoulder when Josh was feeling down, and when Einstein got constipated from too many crickets, Josh gave him warm baths to, um, move things along. Although I didn't feel thrilled at the thought of taking over Einstein duties (or Einstein's doodies), he was Josh's pet, so I wanted Josh to make the decision about Einstein's future.

"Can I ask you something?" I said as we tossed his Pokemon cards in a bin destined for my brother's younger son, Jordan.

"What?"

"What do you want to do about Einstein?"

"What do you mean?" he said.

"Well, is Einstein a family pet or your pet?"

"He's my pet."

"So, what happens while you're at school?"

"You'll take care of him," he said as though it were a done deal.

I shook my head. "I could. But is that what's best for Einstein? You're not going to be here for nine months out of the year and I don't plan to spend any time in your room while you're away because that would make me cry. And I'm definitely not a fan of giving him warm baths and having him sit on my shoulder. I'm thinking maybe that's not the greatest situation for him."

Josh stopped going through his things and sat on the edge of his bed staring at Einstein through the glass walls of his tank. I recalled that Einstein's first tank was tiny, just like him. As he grew, we kept getting new, bigger tanks to keep up with his expanding size. Finally, when the lizard was as long as my arm, I asked the pet shop owner how much bigger Einstein was going to get.

"He will grow to the size of the tank," he said.

"Got it," I said and turned to Josh. "We're not buying any more tanks."

Josh did not have the same attachment to Einstein that he did to Riley, but Einstein had been a constant in his life for nearly a decade, and with so many things changing for him, I knew it had to be difficult for him to contemplate one more change.

"So, what do you think we should do?" he said, more to Einstein than to me.

"It's your call, Josh," I said. "But I had an idea. I bet Jordan would love to take over for you, and then you'd be able to visit Einstein from time to time."

My sister-in-law and I had already discussed this and she'd assured me that my twelve-year-old nephew would be overjoyed to adopt Einstein.

I just let the idea sit there. I didn't want to push it too hard. Joel and I had made all the decisions through the years over which pets got to be members of our family, and the kids accepted whatever we chose. Although I could make this decision too, I realized that Josh was going off to college and was going to be making lots of decisions for himself while he was there, so why not start now?

I saw him swipe at his eyes with his sleeve and realized that he had chosen to turn away from me and look at the tank so I wouldn't see him cry.

"That sounds like a good idea," he finally said. "I'd like Jordan to take Einstein."

I nodded. "Do you want a hug?" I asked.

"No. I'm good," he said, standing up and thrusting his chin out to remind me that he was nearly eighteen and he didn't need hugs and he doesn't cry over lizards.

"Do you want to drive him over to Jordan's with me to help him get settled?"

"No," he said, resuming his sorting. "Jordan's got this."

"What about Einstein? Do you think he'll need help adjusting?"

"Nope," he said. "He's smart. He'll figure it out. That's why I named him Einstein."

....

I started to notice that the kids were spending less time playing with the dog. I knew it was the natural order of things that they would be home less and out with their friends more, but I still felt bad that Riley seemed to be lying around instead of out swimming with a slew of kids in the pool, or chasing a Frisbee, or following them as they rode their bikes down the block.

"I think Riley is lonely," I said to my husband one night.

"What do you mean?" he asked.

"Well, the kids aren't spending as much time with him and I think he's sad."

"Do you think maybe you're projecting your feelings onto the dog?" he said.

"No," I said defiantly. "Well, maybe."

I thought about it for a moment and suspected my husband was right. Not only didn't the kids want to play with the dog as much, they didn't want to be around me and Joel as much either. And we didn't have nearly as bad gas as the dog did. I got it. I was the same way when I became a teenager, too. But back then, when the Converse sneakers were on the other foot, I figured my parents were happy to have us out of the house. This was around the same time as my younger brother's heavy metal phase, so with him, at least, it made sense.

I knew I was not on board with my kids being absent this soon before they actually left home for good, so I decided to devise a plan.

"We're knocking down a wall in the basement, we're going to paint and carpet it, and put in a big screen TV and a dry bar, and it will be your space for you and your friends," I announced to the kids one night over dinner.

"We are?" said my husband.

"Yes. And then you guys will have a place to hang out with your friends, and Dad I will have to text you to get your okay before we come down."

"We will?" said my husband. "I don't think I was consulted on this."

"Yes, you were. But I think you were sleeping," I said. I looked at the kids and could see their eyes light up. I had just given them the key to the Magic Kingdom.

"There's only one caveat," I said.

They eyed me suspiciously.

"You have to invite Riley to hang out with you, too," I said. At the mention of his name, Riley looked up and walked over to the dinner table to see if anything had dropped on the floor while he was sleeping.

"And when you and your friends go in the pool, the dog gets to swim with you too," I said. "Think of him as your little brother who looks up to you and wants to do what the big kids are doing."

The kids conferred in whispers, blocking us from seeing by shielding their faces with their hands. I could see the wheels turning in their heads as small puffs of air came out of their ears.

"Okay, but what happens if he poops outside when we're in the pool?" said Josh, the chief negotiator.

"You have bag it up when your friends leave," I said.

Josh grimaced. He had a super sensitive sense of smell and sometimes even the sight of Riley's poop would make him gag. I knew this was asking a lot of him, but I thought I had sweetened the pot enough to make it work.

"I'm fine with all of it," said Emily, who was also happy to be included in the plans with the big kids.

"Sounds good to me," said my husband.

"Josh?" I said.

"Just one question," he said. "How big a TV are we talking about?"

....

It always helps expedite a renovation when the kid of your contractor is your son's best friend. The basement got its facelift in record time and the new furniture had just been delivered when suddenly, the grand re-opening hit a snag.

"Hey Mom," Emily yelled from the basement. "Can you come down here?"

"I'm in the middle of something," I yelled back from the office. "Can it wait?"

"No, I don't think so," she said.

I closed my laptop and walked to the basement door. Emily was standing at the bottom with a very concerned look on her face.

"What's up?"

"The ceiling," she said.

"Is that a joke?" I asked.

"Nope. Come take a look."

I went to the bottom of the stairs with Riley at my heels and looked up to where Emily was pointing. At the back of the newly renovated space, just above the new dry bar, the new carpeting, and the new sectional, was a giant paint bubble. It was the size and shape of a blimp and it was hanging down about three feet from the ceiling. I gawked at the sight and then turned to Emily.

"This is not good."

I could tell from looking at it that it was filled with water and I knew right away what had happened. During the renovation, we moved the washer and dryer from the basement up to the breakfast room. The breakfast room was directly over the basement. Somehow, the new plumbing for the washing machine had sprung a leak and water had collected in the ceiling of the basement. And from the looks of it, it was about to un-collect all over the new dry bar, carpeting, and sectional.

"Take the dog and go upstairs," I ordered her.

"Why, what's going to happen?" she asked.

"That big water bubble is going to burst," I said, as I noticed droplets of water start to drip out of the bubble.

"When?"

"Now!" I said, grabbing her arm and Riley's collar and bolting up the basement stairs. Halfway up, we heard a giant whoosh and then an enormous splash. We all stopped, except the dog who, upon hearing the sound, decided that giant bursting water bubbles were even less appealing than robotic vacuums and helium balloons, and he ran the rest of the way up the stairs with his tail between his legs.

There are some places where it's good to have water. Water in the coffee maker is good. Water in the bathtub is good. Water in the basement . . . not so much. Especially after you've spent a lot of money on said basement.

Emily and I tiptoed down the stairs, as though we were trying not to disturb what I assumed was our new indoor pool. I took one look and my heart sank.

"Should we get some towels to clean it up?" asked Emily.

"I appreciate your willingness to help, Em, but this is a major deal. We're going to need the mother of all towels and a crew to clean this up."

I shook my head and went back up the stairs. There was no point in even attempting to handle this myself. I picked up the phone and called Joel.

"We had a leak in the ceiling of the new basement," I said.

"How bad?" he wondered.

"Think Niagara Falls."

"Call the plumber," he ordered.

"This is beyond the plumber, honey. I think we need FEMA to come help with this."

"You call the contractor and I'll call the insurance company," he said. "Can you take some pictures of the ceiling and the damage, too?"

"Sure," I said. I ran upstairs to my bedroom to make a quick bathroom stop before I went back to the scene of the crime. But when I got to the bathroom, I discovered another issue.

"The toilet is leaking," I told Joel when I called him a second time. I turned the water off behind the toilet, so the emergency was on hold, but I was drenched.

"Are you kidding me?" he demanded.

"Honey, I have water in the basement and water in the bathroom. I'm soaking wet and the dog is swimming upstream. I wouldn't kid about this."

"Did you call the contractor yet?" he asked.

"No, it's raining outside so I was waiting to see if the roof leaked."

"Mom," shouted Emily from the floor below when I hung up. "Can you come back down here?"

I really did not want to go back down there. I would have paid good money not to go back down there . . . although things up here were not that rosy, either. I took a deep breath and went down to the main level. Emily stood at the top of the basement stairs looking at a trail of water that ran up from the basement and out the length of the hall runner. We followed the water trail to the family room where we found a wet carpet and Riley, soaking wet, chillin' like a villain on the family room sofa. Apparently, he decided swimming in the basement was on his Top Ten List of Things to Do, and not climbing on the furniture was a rule you only followed when your house was not in a flood zone.

I shook my head and shooed the dog off the couch.

"So, are we going to get new furniture?" said Emily, already moving on from the whole ordeal.

"Probably," I said and then glared at Riley.

"And a new dog, too."

....

Before we brought Riley home, the breeders put a yellow ribbon around his neck because he was an easy-going puppy, and they called him Mellow Yellow. But from the moment we swapped out his ribbon for a collar, he changed from the quiet wallflower to the class clown. His favorite place was in the middle of everything and if he couldn't be a part of our party, then he would make his own party. Whenever the kids had friends over to swim, he swam with them. When we played a family board game, he sat next to us, or more typically, on the board game itself. When I announced that it was time to go to school, he would be the first one at the door.

We kept thinking he would get mellower as he got older, but it never happened. He had no time for mellow. There were too many

Frisbees to catch, too many squirrels to chase, too many people to meet. He had friends and fans everywhere . . . from the groomer to the pet store owner to his "other" mommy, who cared for him when we went away. Even the teller at the bank drive-thru knew him by name and would give him a treat along with my money when we stopped by. It was hard to ignore him. Wherever he went he announced his arrival as he busted in through the door and barked hello to let everyone know he was there. No matter where he went, a chorus of "Hey Riley!" would always greet him. The old friends knew the exact spot just above his tail where he liked to be scratched. The new friends figured it out as he pushed his way between their legs and then stopped halfway through so he would be in perfect scratching position.

I knew he was friendly, but I'd had my doubts about how smart he was. He failed Puppy Kindergarten, tripped up steps, and would routinely run into the glass door leading to the backyard, rarely stopping to see if it was actually open. But then I realized he was merely his own dog who didn't have time for rules like "stay" or closed doors that got in his way. When he heard the electric grind of the garage door go up at the end of the day, he knew Dad was home and he would go get the Frisbee and wait impatiently by the door. He knew the word "pool" meant a chance to swim, and "bath" was something to avoid at all costs. The day I came downstairs and saw him step on the pedal of the new garbage can to raise the lid so he could get a snack, I knew the dog might actually qualify for membership in Mensa.

All seemed to be right in Riley's world. And then one day I took him to the vet for a routine physical. Unlike most dogs, Riley was never afraid of the vet's office, most likely because he was always greeted enthusiastically by the front desk people who showered him with little doggie treats. Even in the office, he didn't balk when he was lifted onto the cool metal examining table where he would wait patiently for whatever came next. At times like these I thought about when Emily was little and had to go to the doctor. She would start screaming even before she got into the car and wouldn't stop until we left the office. I always thought it was too bad that some petting and a few chicken treats didn't have the same effect on her as they did on the dog.

When Dr. Benson entered the examination room, Riley greeted her like an old friend. Of course, he greeted everyone like an old friend, but Dr. Benson was special to him, and I'm pretty sure she felt the same way.

"Okay, shots look up to date. His weight is pretty good," she said, looking at his chart. "So, how old is Riley?"

"He's ten," I told her.

"Hey, you're almost an old man," she said to him as she stroked his head.

"Shh," I said. "Don't say that. He doesn't know!"

"Well, let's see how he's doing." She ran her hands around certain parts of his body and then manipulated his back legs.

"He's definitely got some arthritis in his hips," she said. "Have you noticed him limping at all?"

"Just at the end of the day sometimes after he's done a lot of running to chase the Frisbee," I said. "I just figured he was sore."

"Let's put him on glucosamine to help with the joints. Does he do anything besides run after the Frisbee?"

"He still loves to swim in the pool," I said. At the mention of the word *pool*, the dog's ears perked up and he looked around to see where I had put it.

"That's great for his joints," she said. "Keep that up."

"What about in the winter?" I said.

"Maybe you can get him a wetsuit?" she said and winked at me.

I took Riley home and brought him outside to play. I noticed for the first time that the short black hairs around his mouth and nose were beginning to gray. Some white hairs had sprouted around his eyes, as well. Even his body had begun to change. He had what could best be described as a middle-aged "dad" bod — thickening around the middle and a little droopy in the shoulders. I wondered how I could have missed this, and then realized I had probably been too unnerved watching my kids getting older to focus on the subtle changes in the dog's appearance. The kids were five and seven when we got the dog and now they were fifteen and seventeen. They had changed dramatically in those ten years, as kids are wont to do, but the one constant had always been the dog. Riley was Riley no matter what age the kids were or what stage of life they were in. It felt like it had always been that way and always would.

Now I could see change coming. Time was racing by. Josh would be off to college soon and then Emily two years later. Before we knew it, Joel and I would be empty nesters. It was all happening too fast and it seemed like making sure the dog stayed well was critically important now. I needed him to be okay so I could pretend that life wasn't about to hurl me forward into a stage I wasn't ready for yet, and didn't want. Because it wasn't just Riley who was getting old. So was I.

....

A few months later spring arrived and our backyard erupted into a breathtaking botanical garden. It seemed like overnight the trees had all sprung to life and the sweet smell of magnolias filled the air. I took in the view from my back deck and I inhaled deeply as though it would clear out any negative thoughts I had and wipe out the stale smell of winter. Riley kept me company while the kids were at school and I filled barrel planters with geraniums and vinca vines. We had reopened the pool over the weekend and while it was too cold for us to swim, Riley dove right in.

I was filled with the joy of renewal that had been dormant for six months. But there was one thing that made me pause. Even with the glucosamine tablets, Riley's limping had become more pronounced. He was having trouble coming down the stairs and was spending more time lying on the floor than playing outside. When he did go outside to chase a ball, he walked instead of ran. He reminded me of my grandfather who, in a matter of months, went from playing golf every day, to watching golf on TV, to forgetting what golf even was. By the time Riley refused to go up the stairs one night, I knew that something was clearly wrong with him and he needed to get checked out.

I brought him back to the vet, and when Dr. Benson lifted him onto the examining table and put her arms back near his hips, he yelped. It was the first time I'd ever heard him cry out in pain, and I winced. Once he was on the table, though, he seemed fine. Dr. Benson felt around his abdomen and back near his hips. She scowled as she examined him and I got a sinking feeling in my stomach.

"I'm feeling something down here," she finally said. "I'd like to do an x-ray just to rule some things out, okay?"

I nodded and decided I didn't want to ask any "what do you think?" or "what if" questions. While they took Riley into the back, I took a seat on the bench next to a woman with a French Bulldog in a cone of shame and a shaved inner thigh. The plaintive cries of cats waiting in their carriers joined in with the distant barks of dogs being examined in the back. Cute animal posters lined the walls and the Christmas photo greeting cards from the office "patients" still hung from the front desk even though Christmas had long since passed. I could feel the warmth of fear creep into my face as I began the denial process. Riley was only ten. His breed usually lived at least until twelve, sometimes fourteen. Whatever he had going on probably wasn't life threatening. Even if it was something like a mass, they'd remove it. Or shrink it. Or kill it off with drugs. I'd had friends with older dogs who'd had all sorts of health issues. Cancer, diabetes, kidney problems. They found ways to treat what was wrong, extending the dogs' lives for years. Although Riley had seen his fair share of vet visits, I was certain this was just going to be a bump in the road.

But when Dr. Benson called me back into the examination room, I could see on her face that this wasn't going to be a bump. It was going to be a sinkhole.

Riley bounded over to me as though we hadn't seen each other in two weeks, instead of two hours. If it hadn't been for the limp, I would have thought he was fine, but Dr. Benson didn't let me wonder about it too long. One of the things I'd always loved about her was that she was direct and to the point. Or maybe that was just how she was with me. At that moment, though, I thought I could use a little sugar-coating. But none came.

"Riley has some kind of mass in his abdomen," she said. "Unfortunately our office isn't equipped to fully determine the extent of his problem."

"So, what do we do?" I asked, absentmindedly petting the pronounced "smart bump" on his head.

"There's a place about an hour south of here where we refer all of our clients when their pet has something more serious going on. They are wonderful doctors and they'll take really good care of Riley."

"Okay, I'll call for an appointment," I said.

"Actually, we'll call and let them know you're coming, but I think you should take him there now."

The urgency she conveyed now had me more worried than ever. I tried to focus on the instructions she gave me so my thoughts didn't go to the worst possible outcome. Dr. Benson gave me directions and then pulled me into a hug. It was the hug more than anything that nearly brought me to tears.

I quickly paid and piled Riley into the car to set off for the specialty animal hospital. Once we were on our way I felt the tears spill over and found myself crying so hard I had to pull over twice to dry my eyes so I could see where I was going. When I got to the hospital parking lot, I called Joel to let him know what was going on.

"So, they found a mass but they don't know what it is or how extensive it is?" he said after I told him everything I knew.

"Yes, but Dr. Benson seemed very concerned so I'm really worried."

"Don't go there yet, honey. She's probably just being conservative to make sure he gets the best possible treatment for whatever's going on."

I started to cry again.

"I'm really scared," I said.

"I get it. Me too. You know what, I'm going to quickly wrap things up here and come be with you. I don't think I could concentrate on work right now anyway."

"Okay," I said. "I didn't want to ask you to leave, but I could use your support right now."

"I know. I'll be there as soon as I can."

....

Riley was brought in to be examined before Joel arrived, and as I sat in the waiting room with the other pet parents, I looked around and saw many faces drawn with the same fear that I felt. By the time the vet had some answers, Joel was there, and the two of us held hands as we were brought into her office to talk.

"Riley has a mass in his abdomen that is wrapped around his spine, and unfortunately, there is no way to remove it without leaving him paralyzed," she said softly. "It's also a very risky surgery and at his age I'm not sure he would even survive it. I'm very sorry."

I blinked repeatedly, unable to say anything in response. We hadn't really known what to expect, but this news was worse than we had both imagined. Except for the slight limp, Riley had almost completely hidden the extent of the pain he was probably in.

"What would you like to do?" she asked us.

"Can we talk about it?" Joel said.

"Of course. I'll let you have the office for a bit."

She walked out and briefly put her hand on my shoulder as she left. I couldn't imagine doing her job and having to go through this with so many families. I had the fleeting thought that veterinarians were remarkable people and I was so grateful for the ones who had been in Riley's life.

We had barely started talking when the vet reappeared.

"We have a new situation," she said. "Riley has developed something called bloat. Basically, the dog's stomach flips on itself and it is life threatening. It's also very painful and we would need to do surgery right away to fix it."

"Could you do the surgery on the mass at the same time?" said Joel.

She shook her head. "No. It would be two separate surgeries."

"What should we do?" I said, turning to Joel, crying anew.

He shook his head and I saw his face crumble. I've seen Joel cry only a handful of times over the past twenty years and the sight of him breaking down, and the knowledge of our impossible choice, filled me with such sorrow all I could do was hold him and cry along with him. He finally grabbed a tissue off the doctor's desk and we faced each other, holding hands, knowing what the answer was. For ten years, Riley had called the shots, but now it was our turn to make the last call, and it was heartbreaking to do.

"We need to call the kids and have them drive down here," Joel finally said, wiping his eyes.

I nodded. I couldn't speak. I was overwhelmed with how suddenly this had all happened. Only five hours had passed since I found out Riley had a problem, and it was almost too much to process. I was heartbroken, but more than anything I was devastated that my kids would have to experience this heartbreak too. From the moment you get a dog, you know this day will come, but you have to hope it won't be for a long time and have a certain amount of denial that it won't ever happen at all. In between, you fill every day with as much love and joy as you can give that dog, so you can try to match the love you know he has for you.

The doctors told us they had sedated Riley and made him as comfortable as they could while we waited for the kids to arrive. I hated having Josh and Emily there to do this with us, but at the same time I knew that being together as a family when the time came was what we needed to do. We had loved him together from the day he came into our home. We would say goodbye together, too.

Cliché as it sounds, a reel of Riley's life ran through my head . . . snapshots of him as a puppy peeing down the hotel hallway, stepping on the garbage can lever to get the goods inside, jumping off the diving rock to get the Frisbee in the pool, sitting around a board game as the four of us played because he knew he was a member of the family, too. I thought about all the times when the kids went to school and it was just Riley and me, both of us just passing time until the kids came home and we could all play. He was present for all of it — the scavenger hunts, the pool parties, the sad times when one of the fish went belly up, and the celebrations when one of the kids scored a goal, or won an award, got a lead part in a show, or simply had a really good day. He was always, reassuringly there, always ready to shower us with love.

When the kids arrived, their eyes were already red from crying. There wasn't much to say. Emily came to me and I engulfed her in a hug while Josh stood apart, unsure how to handle his feelings in front of us. Joel went to Josh and put his arm around him and finally Josh cried, as though his father had given him the permission he needed to let it all out.

It wasn't long before the vet came out and called us into the examination room. It was the first time Joel and I had seen Riley since we'd brought him in, and it was shocking to see this dog who was so full of life before suddenly with little life left in him. He lay on the table with his head down and his eyes droopy and unfocused from the pain medication. It broke my heart.

The doctor gave us a few moments alone with Riley, and then came back in and nodded to us that it was time. We gathered around him and stroked him gently and let him know how much he was loved.

"Riley you are such a good boy," said Joel.

"You're the best boy," said Josh through his tears. Emily lay her head on his belly and cried. I buried my face in his neck and whispered in his ear, "I love you buddy. You have been the best dog ever. You loved us with everything you had. But it's okay . . . We'll be okay. You can go." Riley gave us one last tail thump, and then he was gone.

Riley left us with so many gifts and so many wonderful memories that we knew the pain of losing him would mellow over time, even though the dog, thankfully, never did.

....

For nearly a decade I'd played mom to a brood that transformed from puppy to dog and children to teens, without benefit of an early warning system to signal that these life-altering transitions were about to take place. Every stage brought challenges, rewards, and joy that I never could have predicted, but there was also a reassuring, albeit mostly uncoordinated, rhythm to our hectic lives. The dog's death was the first sign that our little orchestra, if not disbanding, was reorganizing and that my role as its conductor was changing.

Riley and the kids grew up together. They practiced soccer together, they learned to swim together, and they got pink eye at the same time. I had three kids rather than two, although one had four legs. Much as I wanted to freeze time, ten years later it was inevitable that they would all begin the process of leaving.

Of course, none of this was on my mind when Joel and I got married. We knew someday we'd have kids and someday we'd get a dog. Eventually those things came to be and while we were in it, it felt like it would stay that way forever. But somewhere along the line, we forgot that kids grow up and that dogs get old, and when that happens, it is dizzying in its swiftness and its sorrow.

That night, we ordered dinner in and the kids asked if they could take their food upstairs to eat in their rooms. I knew they were probably hurting even more than Joel and I were. They had not only lost their oldest friend that day, but they had also lost a bit of their innocence. Although I wanted us all to grieve together and laugh at the antics that made Riley so uniquely his own dog, I sensed that the kids preferred to be alone, or at least away from us while they sought comfort from their friends via text. It was hard to grasp that Joel and I were no longer the most important people in their lives. At least that was the case for now, anyway. But as I watched my kids disappear upstairs to their rooms, I realized that this was probably our last hurrah. Today they went to their friends for comfort. Later they would go to their partners or spouses for comfort. It was a hard fact of life to swallow as a parent, especially on the heels of losing our dog.

Joel and I took our plates outside to the back deck and ate silently, each lost in our own thoughts. Eventually, I gazed up from where I sat in a weathered Adirondack chair and noticed a full moon beaming down on our backyard.

"I feel like barking at the moon," I finally said, breaking the silence. "You know, in Riley's honor."

"You think he'd hear you?" said Joel, following my gaze up to the moon suspended in the night sky.

"I don't know," I said. "But the neighbors certainly would." I smiled. It felt good to smile after such a painful day.

"You know what that phrase, *barking at the moon* means?" he said.

"No, not really."

"It means to do something in vain," he said.

I sat and thought for a moment.

"I think that fits," I finally said.

"How so?"

"Well, I want to hold on to this moment in our lives," I said. "I want to keep the kids from getting any older so they don't leave and we don't become empty nesters and I don't lose my main purpose in life."

"Well, that's not going to happen," he said.

"I know. I'm barking at the moon."

"I guess you are," he replied.

"I also want to keep them from the pain of losing Riley," I said.

"You can't do that either," said Joel.

"I know. But I wish I could."

The truth was, our kids were no longer children; they were on the cusp of adulthood. And just like I couldn't stop the dog from dying, I couldn't stop my kids from growing up, going off to college, and beginning their new lives without me constantly by their sides to comfort and guide them through the gauntlet of tradeoffs we make along the road to adulthood. It was going to be a thrilling, scary, amazing, and confusing new chapter for them, but I knew if I had done my job right, they would be okay, and I would be okay too, after a time.

AND SO IT BEGINS AGAIN

When Riley passed, I couldn't imagine the day when I could even think about getting a new dog. I was so completely heartbroken by his loss that I could do nothing but grieve. Everything I did, everywhere I went in the house reminded me of the dog. From the back door where he would greet me with his tail wagging his whole body, to the crunchy spot on the family room rug that was his go-to place to throw up . . . the whole house was full of Riley.

Of course, there is no such thing as replacing a beloved pet after you've lost one. But at some point, you realize you still have a lot of room in your heart to love another and once you're done grieving, you might find yourself suddenly open to the idea of getting a new dog.

That was not the case with me. I took the loss of Riley hard and a month later when his ashes were delivered to the front door, I felt an overwhelming sadness all over again. The whole family still felt the loss so deeply, so we decided to do something special for closure. My dad, who was an artist, painted a silhouette of a black dog on a large flat rock. We bought a small dogwood bush and dug a garden out back. Then we planted the bush, added Riley's ashes to the soil, and marked the location with the rock. A year later, the bush had doubled in size and we knew it was Riley's way of watching over us.

About two months after Riley had passed, my kids brought up the idea of another dog.

"I just can't, you guys," I said. "I'm still so sad. Maybe we'll consider it again next summer."

"But Mom, I'm leaving for college next fall," said Josh. "If we don't get a puppy this year, he will never know me. I'll be a stranger to him."

I felt my heart tug. On the one hand, I didn't know if I was ready to let another dog fill the hole in my heart left there by Riley's death. On the other, I sympathized with Josh's desire to be a part of the new dog's life. I let it mull around in my head for a while and by the time the first leaves of autumn began to fall, I felt I was on board.

The husband? Not so much.

"Do you remember how much work a new puppy is?" he asked.

"No, actually, I don't," I admitted, thinking that having a puppy was kind of similar to giving birth. You remember that it hurt a lot, but you can't exactly recall what it felt like, which is why, I guess, people have more children, and get more puppies. "It's been nearly eleven years since we had a puppy and fifteen years since we had a baby. And honestly, I don't even remember what I had for breakfast two hours ago."

He shook his head. "You have to get up in the middle of the night and take them out, and they pee all over the house for months, and they chew up all the furniture, cabinets, and basically everything except the rubber chew toys they are supposed to chew on instead.

"They eat yarn and have to have surgery," he continued more

seriously. "They get a face-full of ticks, they get pink eye and swimmer's ear, and they make you completely fall in love with them so that ten years later you get your heart broken all over again."

I nodded. Four months after Riley had passed, Joel was still hurting. I knew we both had more love to give and I thought I was ready to do that now, but he wasn't sure he was. It was clear I had to give him more time to work through his grief, but I was also aware that time was passing for Josh, and it was important to him, if we were going to get another dog, that he have a chance to be a part of it.

The problem was, once I had the inkling I might want a puppy again, I googled "puppies" and was hypnotized by pages upon pages of cute puppy pictures. It was like crack for puppy lovers. If I had any reservations about the timing, they were immediately rendered null and void by hundreds of photos of wide-eyed puppies looking for homes. I drank the puppy Kool-Aid and I was sold.

Two weeks later I talked to Joel again. This time, for whatever reason, he was able to dive deep into his heart, get past the sadness, and say yes.

We began researching breeds and breeders, adoptions, and rescues but were having trouble seeing ourselves with any dog except a retriever.

Then one day I ran into someone walking an English Cream Golden Retriever and I fell in love for a second time. Her dog was like an all-white version of Riley. The circumstances were so similar to when we'd decided to get Riley that I thought it couldn't be a coincidence. I asked and she gave me the name of her breeder, and then I made the call.

"I found our puppy," I announced to Joel that night after telling him the story of the woman with the English Golden Retriever. "And I know that it was meant to be."

"Oh really?" he said. "How's that?"

"Well this Golden Retriever breeder just had a litter and the puppies will be ready to come home at the end of November, which is perfect for us."

"Is that it?" he said.

"No. It turns out she knows me. Or at least knows of me. Her local newspaper carries my column and she's very familiar with it," I said.

"So, she's a fan?" he asked.

"Not exactly," I mumbled. "She actually uses my column as wee-wee pads for the puppies."

"That's okay, honey," said my husband, taking my hand. "So will we."

ACKNOWLEDGMENTS

There are so many people to thank who have inspired me, supported me, nudged me and told me I am the funniest thing since sliced bread (which is kind of a strange phrase because who knew bread was funny?). I'm sure I will inadvertently forget someone if I try to list you all, so I apologize right now if I leave anyone out because, truly, I love you all and would buy you a lifetime of chocolate for supporting me if I could.

First, I must say thanks to all my friends in the Erma Bombeck Writer's Workshop, especially Teri Rizvi, for your wit, wisdom, and friendship for the past fifteen years! Teri, you have been such a huge supporter, and I'm so grateful to have had you in my corner! Thank you as well to the Bombeck family, Matt, Betsy, and Andy. I only see you every two years, but when I do, you welcome me with open arms, big smiles, and lots of stories over the great Dayton hotel desserts!

To my newspaper editors, Lisa Glowinski, Michael Toesset, and Brett Freeman, and your staff — thank you for allowing me to enter the homes of your subscribers each week in the hopes that I can make them laugh and forget, for a moment, all the craziness in the world.

Much gratitude to my online friends and my Lost in Midlife fan page followers and Facebook group, especially Karen Brill for taking charge while I whipped this puppy into shape. And my real-life friends, Michelle Markovitz, Ed Catallo, Susan Sparks, Dana Stone, and Dan and Hope Sherman, for listening to me whine about how busy I am while I'm truly grateful to be so busy.

I owe a debt of gratitude to Steven Aguiar and Ella Evans, as well as Silvana Bardi and Johanna Colocho from BlueWing Digital for their social media expertise and helping me bring my visions for the Lost in Midlife brand and this book to life. And big congrats to Steven and Ella on the arrival of their tiny new BlueWing boss.

To the members of Jen Louden's Mastermind, Weekly Oasis, and the writers who joined me in a series of retreats, you all taught me to dig deeper and also that it's okay to take a break from writing to dance. And to Jen Louden, our fearless leader, so, so, so much gratitude. A hundred thank yous for your guidance, expertise, and uncanny way of knowing what I was feeling before I did and making sure I got that into my book.

I have to give some hometown love to the great people of New Providence, New Jersey, especially the folks at the old Village Pet Shop who kept us in dog chews, crickets, and goldfish, Jimmy and Harry Vardas for keeping me in French Fries while I wrote this book, Mayor Al and his lovely wife Christine Morgan for being part of my pep squad the entire time we lived in the community, Captain Anthony Buccelli and the New Providence police department for looking the other way when I drove my pets around town in my bathrobe. And so much gratitude for the wonderful, amazing doctors at our local vets for taking such good care of Riley through the years. Much love to Dawn Troutman for loving Riley so much and taking such good care of him when we would go away, and Jacqueline Hasenkopf, along with Christopher, Maddy, Benjamin, and David for making Monty always feel so welcome and loved in your home. And to my neighbors, Rich and Jody, thank you for looking the other way when Riley ran across the fence to poop in your front yard.

Special thanks to my writer friends who I hardly see but who love me unconditionally and tell me the truth when I screw up. Suzette Martinez-Standring, Gordon Kirkland, Cathryn Michon, Nicole Morgan, Anne Parris, and especially W. Bruce Cameron for his wonderful Foreword . . . you guys rock! Gordon and Bruce, I promise, even if I hit the big time, I will still spit cheese on both of you.

Thank you to Arielle Eckstut of The Book Doctors for giving me great input on my first draft and encouraging me to do it "the right way." And to my agent, Lynn Johnston, thank you for continuing to believe in me as I take a circuitous path to publishing success.

Leslie Schwartz, you are my editing hero, the greatest cheerleader, and a sensitive soul like me. Thank you so much for helping me see the forest through the trees, or more accurately, the dog through the fur. This book would not be what it is without you.

Thank you to David Endris and the talented staff at Greenleaf Book Group for your patience and expertise, with a special shout out to my Project Manager, Lindsay Bohls; Executive Editor, Jessica Choi; Marketing Strategist, Emily Maulding; Distribution Account Coordinator, Tiffany Barrientos; and the coolest ever Design Supervisor, Chase Quarterman, who made book cover magic happen for this book.

A huge thanks also to Dan Smith and Corrine Moulder at Smith Publicity and my unbelievable publicist, Janet Shapiro, who is a force of nature, and Shelby Kisgen, who tirelessly helped me get this book into the light. Janet, you are amazing and may be the only person on the planet who makes me feel like I'm standing in place.

Curtis Staropoli and Killian Lennon at Toan Digital, you guys came from nowhere and then gave me the perfect website to help launch this book. Thank you so much for changing the oranges to yellow at my whim and bringing together the book and the site so seamlessly.

To all my author friends who immediately said yes when I asked them to write a blurb for my book, Susan Sparks, Matt Bombeck, Jenny Gardner, Anna Lefler, Leighann Lord, Jenna McCarthy,

Robin Gorman Newman, Susan Konig, Susan Reinhardt, Marcia Kester Doyle, Dawn Weber, Katrina Kittle, Cathryn Michon, Cindy Ratzlaff, V. C. Chickering, Jenny Gardiner, Rebecca Regnier, Joel Madison, and James Breakwell, thank you for taking the time to write such glowing reviews!

To Cait Freaney, who not only loved and helped us care for Riley but also fed crickets to Einstein when we went away. By the way, Cait, there are still some crickets in the vents.

To Julie Minogue, who never knew Riley but loves dogs as much as we do and listened when I cried while writing this book.

Thank you to Victor, Kate, and Marsha for being my legal eagles! I'd much rather have you in my corner than the other guy's.

To my extended family — Harvey, Carol, Nancy, Steve, David, Rich, Paula, Wendy, Karen, Ken, and Jess — thank you for encouraging me to continue on this path, for smiling when I write about you, and for looking the other way when you knew that I was spinning yarns.

Finally, to Joel, Josh, and Emily — you are last in my acknowledgments but first in my heart! You guys are my world! I love you so, so much. You were the best family Riley could have had, and he loved you all right up to the end. I'm thrilled we will always have this book to remember the best dog ever! I couldn't have done it without your love and support and laughter . . . even though I was the one who had to clean up the yard.

ABOUT THE AUTHOR

TRACY BECKERMAN is an Emmy® award-winning author, speaker, and syndicated humor columnist who has appeared on numerous TV shows, including NBC's *The Today Show*, *CBS Sunday Morning*, and *Good Day New York*, talking about marriage, motherhood, and her refusal to drive a minivan. Tracy is also the author of the humor books, *Lost in Suburbia: A Momoir: How I Got Pregnant, Lost Myself, and Got My Cool Back in the New Jersey Suburbs* and *Rebel without a Minivan: Observations on Life in the 'Burbs.*

CPSIA information can be obtained
at www.ICGtesting.com
Printed in the USA
LVHW041630220721
693425LV00003B/351

9 781632 993939